RAJIV D. KHATLAWALA is a Chartered Accountant and a Cost Accountant by profession. Schooled in Mumbai, he graduated from Bombay University in 1988 after which he moved to Baroda, Gujarat, where he acquired both his professional degrees.

Rajiv has more than two decades of experience, including working in industry, as a financial markets trainer, and as a corporate consultant assisting companies in equity research, wealth management, and currency and commodities hedging. His approach to investing is a combination of detailed fundamental analysis and technical analysis.

Rajiv is also an active academician. He is a visiting faculty for the MBA program of the M. S. University of Baroda and also for the G. H. Patel Institute of Management, Vallabh Vidyanagar. He teaches a course on Securities Analysis and Portfolio Management, as well as subjects such as Financial Management and Management Accounting. He has also taught students of ICWAI and ICAI as well.

He is now an independent personal finance and financial markets trainer, providing practical hands-on training in technical analysis, company valuations, and derivatives trading.

Rajiv Khatlawala lives with his mother, his wife and two children in Baroda, Gujarat, India. He can be contacted by email at rajivkhatlawala@yahoo.co.in

Acclaim for the Book

'A lucid and excellent exposition of technical analysis.'

– Prof. (Dr.) G. C. Maheshwari,
Dean, Faculty of Management Studies
M.S. University of Baroda

'Rajiv Khatlawala's book on technical analysis is perhaps one of the simplest books written so far on such a complex subject. Stock market respects both fundamental and technicals alike. If one could combine both with the help of this book he or she shall certainly understand the market dynamics in the right perspective.'

– Jagdish Thakkar, former President,
Vadodara Stock Exchange Ltd.

'The book explains the complex concepts of technical analysis in such a lucid manner that even a lay reader can follow the subject easily. The use of relevant Indian examples throughout the book makes it easier for the reader to relate to the concepts.'

– C.A. Maulik C. Mehta, Chief Executive,
Infinity Consultants Ltd. and an active investor

How to Profit from Technical Analysis

A Beginner's Guide

Rajiv D. Khatlawala

www.visionbooksindia.com

www.visionbooksindia.com

Disclaimer

Investing and trading invariably involve some risk. The author and the publisher disclaim all legal or other responsibilities for any losses which readers may suffer by investing or trading based on information provided in this book, which is meant only for educational purpose. Readers are advised to seek professional advice and guidance before making any trades or investments.

First Published 2008
Reprinted 2008 (Thrice), 2009, 2010, 2011, 2013, 2014
2nd Revised and Enlarged Edition, 2016, 2018, 2020, 2021, 2022, 2023

ISBN 10: 81-7094-959-9
ISBN 13: 978-81-7094-959-6

Published by
Vision Books Pvt. Ltd.
(Incorporating Orient Paperbacks & CARING imprints)
24 Feroze Gandhi Road, Lajpat Nagar 3
New Delhi 110024, India.
Phone: (+91-11) 2984 0821 / 22
e-mail: visionbooks@gmail.com

Printed at
Ashim Print Line
38/2, 35 & 36 Sahibabad Industrial Area, Ghaziabad
Uttar Pradesh 201010, India.

This book is dedicated to

my loving father,

late Shri Dinesh J. Khatlawala,

who,

more than twenty-five years ago,

insisted that for long term success

the financial markets must be approached

scientifically and not arbitrarily.

'Most traders and investors like to think of themselves as risk-takers, but what they really want is a guaranteed outcome with some momentary suspense.'

– Mark Douglas

Contents

Preface

'Mr. Market is always right.'
– Anon.

The global financial markets today influence a majority of the world's population far more emphatically than was the case, say, even fifty years back. Among the market economy countries, a large proportion of their population invests in the security markets. Financial powerhouses every year recruit growing numbers of management graduates into this field, not to mention the many who find their way into the financial jungle through other routes — as agents, brokers, advisors, etc.

While a majority of investment and finance professionals have been introduced, exposed and trained in carrying out fundamental research of companies, industries and economies, not many are well versed with the second and relatively lesser-known field of technical analysis.

Even a decade ago most of today's fund managers and finance professionals would have shunned technical analysis as mere mumbo-jumbo. But perceptions have changed in the recent few years, helped by market crashes, such as the great technology crash.

Market players have woken up to the fact that a mere analysis of corporate annual reports and balance sheets, and calculations of projected figures do not provide a full answer to the investment puzzle, and that there remain some other pieces in the jigsaw to which they must give due importance.

This realization led to a growing number of fundamentalists taking an interest in the study of price behavior, namely technical analysis.

There is an old market saying, 'Mr. Market is always right.' While fundamental analysis often ignores this dictum, technical analysis is based squarely on the assumption that the market is always right. Thus, the basic premise on which this science was built, itself gives it a positive head start.

The purpose of this book is both to create an awareness of the importance and relevance of price behavior and to equip investors and traders with enough basic knowledge and tools to begin using technical analysis in their investment decisions.

I wish all the readers the best of luck and sincerely hope that this book will help them get started in to this exciting profitable field.

RAJIV D. KHATLAWALA

Acknowledgements

I strongly believe that anything worthwhile is created only with the support and guidance of many people.

Right from the conception of this book to the process of writing and reviewing it and finally getting it into your hands, I have been supported, assisted and guided by several people, some close to me and others whom I have only recently met.

I wish to acknowledge that without my mother's blessings this book would have remained but a dream. Also, I particularly wish to thank my wife Parul, who helped sustain my enthusiasm and encouraged me throughout, and my children Adit and Manushi who kept encouraging me.

I wish to specially thank Mr. Kapil Malhotra, Publisher of Vision Books, New Delhi for showing confidence in me right from the beginning as for guiding me on the book's content, layout and style.

I also want to thank my students as also the participants of my workshops on technical analysis who gave me valuable feedback, both positive and otherwise, on my sessions with them. I hope they will be happy to see their feedback incorporated in this book.

Also I take this opportunity to thank Reliable Software Systems Pvt. Ltd, Mumbai for giving permission to use charts and graphs from their Trend charting software in this book.

Last but not the least, I thank the editorial team of Vision Books and the printers for making this book possible.

I know that all of you have made my dream come true will all be there to support me in my subsequent ventures.

List of Abbreviations

DMA	Days' Moving Average
EMA	Exponential Moving Average
FII	Foreign Institutional Investor
HNI	High Net-Worth Individuals
HPCL	Hindustan Petroleum Corporation Limited
ICE	Information-Communication-Entertainment Sector
MTNL	Mahanagar Telephone Nigam Limited
MACD	Moving Average Convergence Divergence
NIFTY	National Stock Exchange Index of Fifty Stocks
NCDEX	The National Commodities and Derivatives Exchange
NYMEX	New York Mercantile Exchange
RSI	Relative Strength Index
SMA	Simple Moving Average
SENSEX	The Bombay Stock Exchange Index of Thirty Stocks
TISCO	Tata Iron and Steel Company Limited
WMA	Weighted Moving Average
Y2K	Year 2000

1

Introduction to Technical Analysis

'Searching the future from the past.'

The Meaning of Technical Analysis

Technical analysis is primarily the scientific study of prices. To be more specific, we can say that it is the study of past price and volume data of a tradable security in order to gauge the likely future direction of its price.

Here, it is important to mention that:

1. Technical analysis pre-supposes that the security being analyzed is actively traded, i.e. its daily or weekly trading volume is reasonably high. Technical analysis may not work effectively in

the case of securities which typically witness erratic and / or scanty trading volumes.

2. Like any other method of analysis, technical analysis is not an exact science; rather, its purpose is to gauge the future direction that the prices are *likely* to take. Since we are trying to project the future, which is necessarily uncertain, one can therefore only talk in terms of probabilities.

3. Concerned as it is with the future, technical analysis is dynamic in nature. Thus any analysis has to be adjusted and modified as new data becomes available. This sort of dynamism also exists in the study of fundamentals but the difference is that the frequency of adjustment and modification is lesser in the latter, thus giving a false notion that fundamental analysis is a surer method of analysis.

The Scope of Technical Analysis

The study of technical analysis can theoretically be applied to any market where its basic raw data, namely information on prices and volumes, is available. Thus, technical analysis can be applied to any financial market where one witnesses price movement on a regular basis and where data is available for the number of transactions (volume).

This has led to technical analysis being very widely used including the foreign exchange markets, the commodities markets, the metals markets, and stock markets as well as in bullion markets the world over. In fact, contrary to popular belief technical analysis is far more widely used by forex and commodity traders, and only more recently by an increasing number of stock traders. Open any website on forex trading and you will find prominent mention of technical analysis on its front page.

Is Technical Analysis a Self-fulfilling Science?

Critics of technical analysis often point out that it is a self-fulfilling science. They argue that since all technical analysts would see the same patterns on a chart they tend to act in similar fashion and their concerted action leads to a particular pattern repeating itself.

While the criticism may not be entirely untrue, it can equally be argued that even many facets of traditional fundamental analysis would also be similarly self-fulfilling in nature.

Moreover, prices are not merely a function of technical patterns but also reflect the basic underlying fundamental news and inputs which continually flow into the markets. The statement then that technical analysis is a self-fulfilling science may only be partially true.

Basic Assumptions Underlying Technical Analysis

Any science and its theories are based on certain assumptions and this is true of technical analysis as well, which is built on the following prominent foundations:

1. The existence of a tradable security for which there is a reasonably large market.

2. The price of the security at any point in time is the sum total of various factors, such as hope, fear, money power, recent news events, current economic situation, and the perception of market players. Thus, the price at a particular time discounts (has built in it) all such information, as well as the sentiment of all the market players at large — whether these be fundamentalists or technical traders, individual investors or large institutional ones.

3. That the market movements are not chaotic; rather, there is an orderly movement in the markets. This is borne out by the fact that markets generally move in trends. Historically, randomness of market movements was accepted but recent perceptions have

changed suggesting an underlying order behind the seemingly chaotic moves of the market. It is often pointed out that 'chaos is not in the markets but in the minds of the trader'.

4. Market players tend to repeat their actions over and over again. Technical analysis therefore holds that price patterns once identified can be traded effectively since market players are likely to repeat their previous reactions in similar future situations. Rightly it is said that 'what we learn from history is that we never learn from history'.

Advantages and Pitfalls of Technical Analysis

There are several distinct advantages of using technical analysis when you are investing or trading in the markets:

1. The study of prices gives one a feel of the direction of price movement. This is more specifically referred to as trend analysis.

2. Technical analysis helps traders and investors alike to review their investment decisions faster. This is because prices tend to discount, i.e. anticipate, fundamental information much before an actual event takes place. The widely accepted market axiom, 'Buy the rumor and sell the fact' reflects this point.

3. Technical analysis brings to bear systematic and often disciplined approach to the investment process. The use of stop loss is a case in point. When traders and investors exit using stop losses, it actually means that the very basis on which they had entered the market seems to have been negated by the market's subsequent reaction in terms of prices. It would thus be better to get out of the market for some time and coolly review the original decision.

4. Technical analysis often gives an advance signal of an impending reversal in the markets. Typically these are times when investor reactions are extreme in nature, irrational exuberance at the top of a bull market, for example, which can take prices way beyond

their fair value. A case in point was the bull run of technology stocks in 1999–2000, and their subsequent fall. During that period many technical indicators gave advance warning of an impending reversal in sentiment.

While there are advantages, there are also bound to be pitfalls, of which some important ones are:

1. Technical analysis is not an exact science. It is the study of a dynamic situation and you must therefore continuously review your decision in the light of fresh price action.

2. The basics of technical analysis may be easy to learn but the nuances are difficult to implement and master. Most traders using this science tend to oscillate between different approaches and thus fail to follow through with their analysis in a consistent and coherent manner. This invariably leads to losses, followed by disillusionment.

Trader *versus* Investor

Readers should note that throughout the book 'short term trading' would mean trading for a few days; 'medium term trading' would mean trading for a few weeks, and 'long term trading' would mean trading for a few months. For the purpose of this book, we have used the terms long term trader and investor interchangeably.

2

Trend Analysis

'The trend is your friend.'

– Old market saying

Types of Price Charts

The Basics of Trends

Types of Trends

Trend Reversal

Drawing Trend Lines on Price Charts

Support and Resistance Lines

The Paradox of Periodicity

The Importance of Volumes

The Dow Theory

Types of Price Charts

Prices of any security can be plotted on a graph paper, in much the same way as we used to make graphs in school. But there are obvious limitations to manual plotting. With the advent of computers and rapid advancement of software programming, however, charts of financial securities traded on major exchanges around the world are now available with great ease and improved visual and manipulation capabilities. Most charting software now provide price charts with many years of data.

It would be appropriate here to look at the various types of price charts.

Charts Based on Time Frame

- **Daily charts** showing a day's open, high, low and closing prices.
- **Weekly charts** showing a week's open, high, low and closing prices. A week is always assumed to start on Monday and end on Friday.
- **Monthly charts** showing a month's open, high, low and closing prices.

Charts Based on Price Depiction

- **Line (or closing) chart** where only the closing price of each day / period is plotted (Chart 2.01).

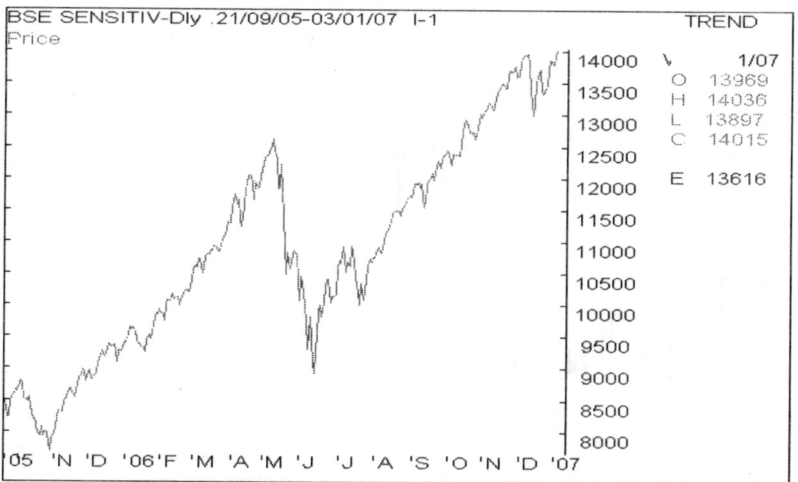

Chart 2.01: **Example of a line or closing price chart**

- **Bar chart** where only the open, high, low and closing prices are plotted in the form of a bar (Chart 2.02).

- **Candlestick chart** where the open, high, low and closing prices are depicted in the form of Japanese candlesticks (Chart 2.03).

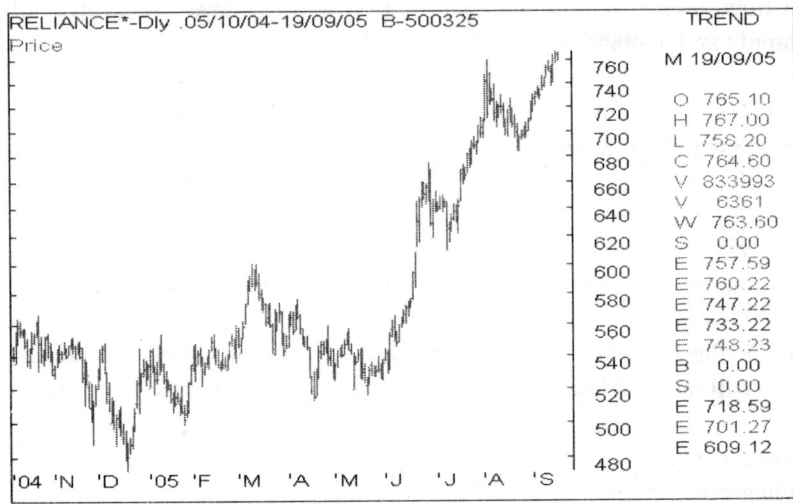

Chart 2.02: **Example of a bar chart**

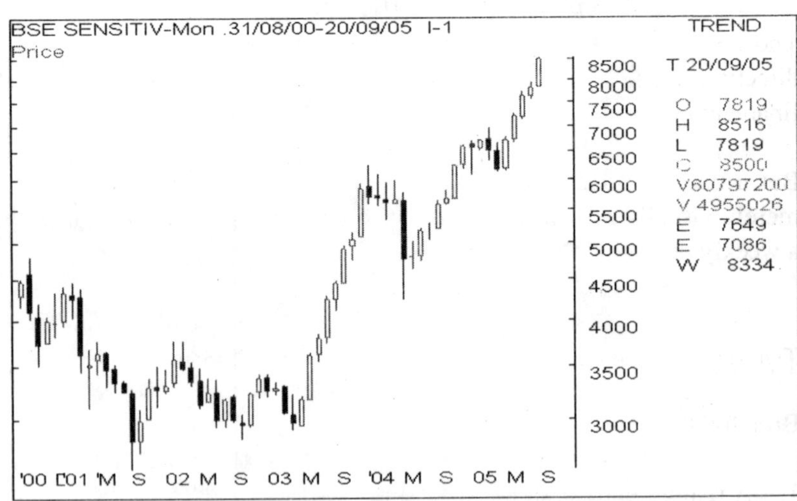

Chart 2.03: **Example of a Japanese candlesticks chart**

The Basics of Trends

Decades of price charts have demonstrated one basic truth — prices move in trends.

A trend indicates that there exists an inequality between the forces of supply and demand:

- When the supply of a stock or commodity is greater than the demand for it, the trend will be down since there are more sellers than buyers;
- When demand exceeds supply, the trend will be up as the more numerous buyers bid up the price; and
- If the forces of supply and demand are nearly equal, the market will move sideways — in what is called a trading range.

A trend may thus be considered as a phase in a market's movement when prices are going in a particular direction, notwithstanding some smaller counter moves in the opposite direction.

Those who don't use price charts can get an indication of the general direction of how prices are moving by regularly following the financial media.

But a user of price charts will be able to get a better idea even by merely visually reviewing the longer time-frame price charts, such as a weekly or a monthly chart.

Types of Trends

Broadly, there may be two types of trends:

1. A rising trend, or an up trend; and
2. A falling trend, or a down trend.

A rising trend, or up trend, is said to exist when prices are generally rising, notwithstanding small intermittent falls (corrections).

To be more specific, **when prices make higher highs and higher lows, it is a case of rising trend.** This must be considered as a basic and necessary condition of an up trend (Chart 2.04).

Chart 2.04: **Example of an up trend. Points H1, H2, H3 and H4 show higher highs while points L1, L2, L3 and L4 are higher lows.**

A falling trend, or a down trend, on the other hand is said to exist when prices are generally falling notwithstanding small up moves (corrections).

More precisely, **when prices make lower highs and lower lows, it is a case of falling trend.** This must be considered as a basic and necessary condition of a down trend (Chart 2.05).

Chart 2.05: **Example of a down trend. Points L1, L2, L3 and L4 show the lower lows while points H1, H2, H3 and H4 indicate lower highs.**

Further, during a rising or a falling trend there may be periods when prices move in a narrow range. On the charts, this would appear as if the price is moving horizontally, i.e. sideways. Such a period is said to be a flat or sideways trend. It may be noted that a sideways trend is not a trend in the real sense of the word, but only a period of non-directional price stagnation also called a trading market as distinct from a trending market.

What's a Correction?

One important point that needs to be made here is that the term correction does not necessarily mean falling prices. It simply means a smaller price move which is counter, i.e. opposite, to the prevailing trend.

Trend Reversal

When the basic and necessary condition defining a trend is invalidated, it is a signal of a trend reversal.

Thus:

- When after consistently making higher highs and higher lows in an ongoing rising trend, the market index or a stock as the case may be, makes a lower high and lower low formation, the up trend is said to have reversed direction into a down trend.

- Conversely, when after consistently making lower highs and lower lows in an ongoing falling trend, the market or a stock makes a higher high and higher low formation, the down trend is said to have reversed direction to up. (See Chart 2.06)

Chart 2.06: **Example of a trend reversal. The latter part of the above chart is a continuation of Chart 2.05 which showed the previous down trend in the same security. Subsequently, the price broke above the most recent high (marked H4) which suggested that the down trend had reversed.**

Knowledge of both the current trend and trend reversal is important for traders and investors for making appropriate trading and investment decisions. Thus:

- In a rising trend, a trader's strategy would be to buy stocks on any price falls (corrections), and then wait for price to resume its up trend.

- Conversely, when the main trend is down, a trader's strategy would be to exit stocks on price rises (corrections), and then wait for lower prices to re-enter the market.

Drawing Trend Lines on Price Charts

Trend lines, as the name suggests, are lines drawn on price charts that visually depict the direction of the trend, and also the likely buying and selling zones. Thus:

- In order to depict an up trend, a trend line is drawn on a price chart by joining the successive higher lows being formed — remember, higher lows being a condition of an up trend as noted earlier.

- Conversely, a down trend line on a price chart is drawn by joining the successively lower highs being formed; lower highs being a basic condition of a down trend as noted earlier.

One aspect to be kept in mind while drawing a trend line is that **it is possible to draw more than one trend line in the same direction.** The only difference would be the 'slope' (angle) of the trend lines. Chart 2.07 shows one main trend line along with three steeper ones.

The steeper a trend line, the less effective it will be as it can be more easily broken by a volatile price movement or, many a time, even by a sideways price movement. It is the less steep trend line (referred to as the main trend line in Chart 2.07) which provides a trader with the more important and reliable price levels.

Trend lines can also help us identify price zones where buying and selling is likely. Let us see how.

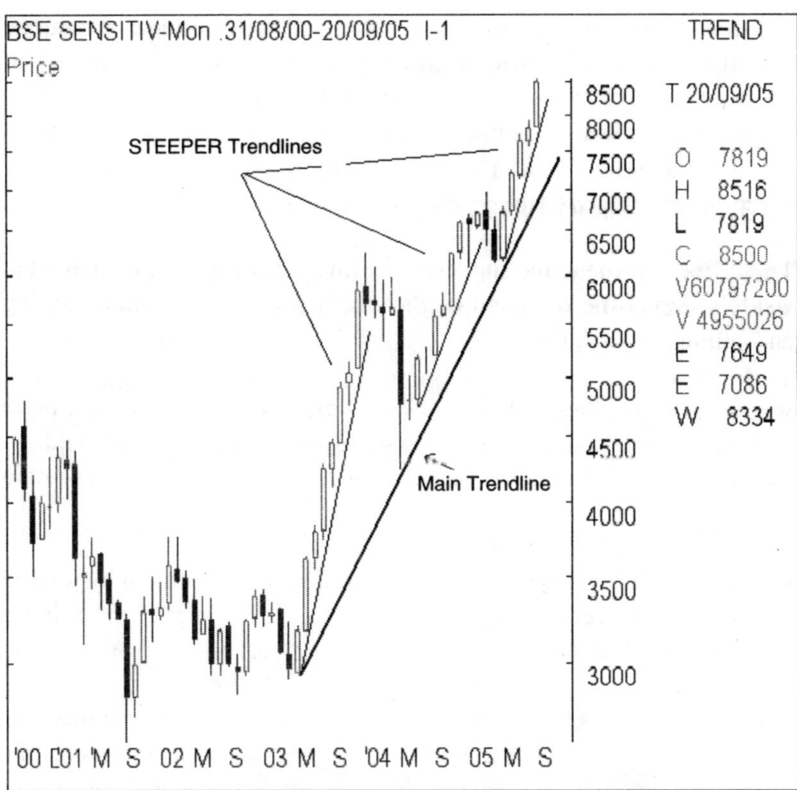

Chart 2.07: **More than one trend line on the same chart. Observe that the main trend line is less steep than the other three, shorter lines. The steeper lines indicate the 'immediate' support level (or resistance as the case may be) while the main line provides you with the major support level (or resistance as the case may be).**

Support and Resistance Lines

A trend line formed by joining the higher lows of an up trend line is also called a support line. These are the price levels where fresh buying interest comes in which leads to the price bouncing back higher. **Prices are likely to find buying support in the vicinity, or around, a support trend line.** This is an important point to grasp since technical analysis is not an exact science. So if a support trend line gives a level of, say, ₹ 325 as a support level for a stock, you should grow alert as the price starts approaching ₹ 325.

Conversely, a down trend line formed by joining the lower highs also acts as a resistance line. The price levels along this line are price points where the stock attracts selling pressure.

Chart 2.08 shows trend lines on a weekly bar chart, which is the weekly bar chart of Wipro Limited. You may note that the resistance line is drawn by joining the successive lower highs of the periods of the down trend while the support line is drawn by joining the successive higher lows of the up trend. You may also observe that breaking of the resistance line by the price gave the signal of a trend reversal.

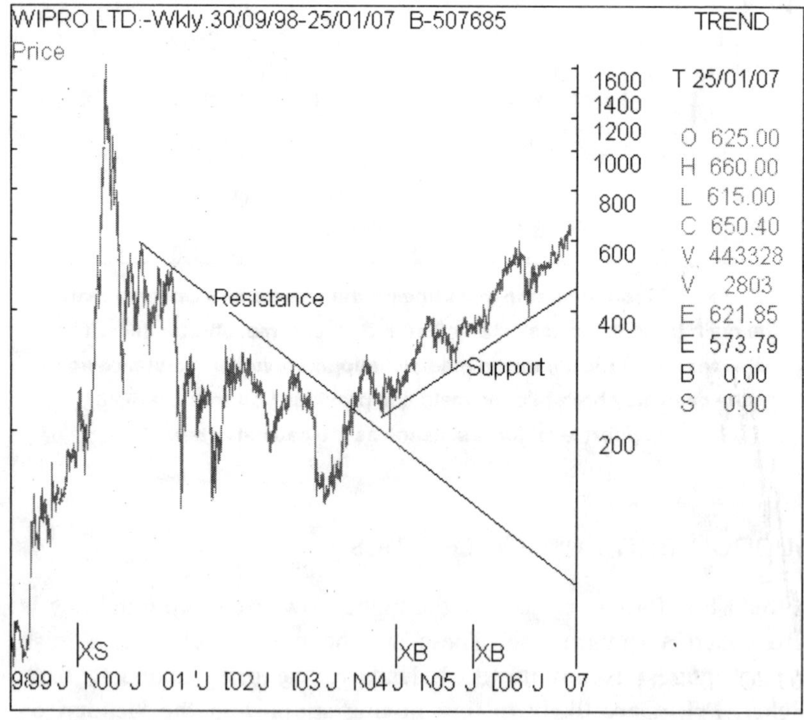

Chart 2.08: **Resistance and support trend lines on the weekly price chart of Wipro**

In the current run up the price is being supported by rising support line and in the process making higher highs and higher lows.

How Support and Resistance Lines Reverse Their Roles

Once an index or share's price breaks through and falls below a support line, prices in the subsequent corrective up move tend to witness selling pressure near what was earlier the defined support line, i.e. the buying area. Thus, the earlier support line, after having been broken, changes into a resistance line when prices try to go up again. Chart 2.09 shows an example of such a role reversal.

Chart 2.09: **Example of role reversal**

Let's try and understand what really happens when a support line is broken. Traders who bought near a support level did so in the belief that prices would bounce back up from there. Once the support line is broken, however, the earlier bets are off and the same traders would exit their positions whenever the price rises back near their buying levels represented by what had earlier been the support line. This then creates a selling pressure near the earlier support line as traders try to exit with minimum possible loss. And this selling pressure at the earlier support line converts it into a new resistance line.

Chart 2.09 of Reliance Industries indicates that the ₹ 490 level was a resistance area for the stock for a long period, in fact, during the entire 2005 and till mid-2006. In June 2006, the price broke the resistance level of 490, rallied to 528 and then fell back to 'test' the 500 levels again. The earlier resistance area of 490-500 had now 'reversed roles' and this area actually became the support area — where there were more buyers than sellers.

The converse holds true in the case of the price breaking through above a resistance line. Thus in any subsequent downward correction after the break, the price tends to find support at what was the earlier resistance line. This is because there would be traders who might earlier have sold near the resistance level, believing that like before the prices would fall back and give them a chance to re-enter at lower levels. However, when they find that the resistance level has been broken and prices have risen above their selling prices, the earlier assumption no more holds true. These traders would now wait for the price to come back again 'near' their selling prices (i.e., the earlier resistance level) to exit their selling position. This then creates a buying pressure near the earlier resistance line as many traders try to exit (in this case, buy back) with the minimum possible loss and the earlier resistance line thus becomes a new support line.

This market behavior is what leads to a role reversal wherein the earlier support level becomes a new resistance, and *vice versa.*

The Paradox of Periodicity

Using price charts presents an important dilemma. What time frame should one use? Should you give importance to the daily charts (which plot the open, high, low and closing price of each day), or should one use a weekly chart (which plots the open, high, low and close of each week's price movement) instead, and so on.

This dilemma is actually a good starting point for any trader or investor to think through a coherent approach to follow. I suggest a two-step approach:

1. First determine whether you want to be an intraday trader, or whether you wish to hold your trading position for a few days, a few weeks — or may be a few months.

2. Once you've decided your basic trading horizon, you can then select the time frame of the price charts accordingly.

Thus, let us suppose you want to take a trading position for the next three to four days. The most logical action would then seem to be to work with the daily chart of the security you are tracking. But my observation has been that this starting point may not be the most prudent one. **If you want to take a trading position for the next three or four days, you must actually choose a lower time frame and analyze the intraday charts, and not the daily chart.**

Similarly if you want to take a trading position for thirty days (four weeks), it would be better that you analyze the daily and not the weekly charts.

The reasoning is simple. If you are taking a three to four day view, the intraday price (say, hourly charts) movements and levels will have a greater bearing on the price movement for your chosen time period than the levels depicted on the daily charts. The daily price charts will take a relatively longer time to reflect the price action of the most recent three to four days, while the intraday price chart (say, the hourly chart) will be quicker in reflecting the relevant price action.

Thus it is almost a paradox. If you are a day-trader you shouldn't actually use the daily charts but the intraday (15-minute, half-hourly or hourly) charts.

The Importance of Volumes

Volume, or the number of underlying securities traded, is an important part of the study of price charts. Volume tells us whether or not there is active market interest in a security. Volume, however, is a relative term. Whether a particular level of volume is high or low depends on the security's normal (average) trading volume, its price, the security's inclusion — or otherwise — in an index, its available floating stock, etc.

Thus, at the time of writing this book (February 2007), for Infosys a volume of ten lakh shares traded in a day would have been considered high, but for ITC, even a volume of more than twenty-five lakh in a day may have been average, or even low.

Let us now understand some basic rules of the relationship between price and volume.

First of all, any price move supported with higher, or increasing, volumes is suggestive of a strong trend. Thus:

- Rising prices along with rising volumes is a bullish (positive) sign; and

- Falling prices along with rising volumes is a bearish (negative) sign.

Conversely, therefore, any price move which is not supported by a volume expansion is suggestive of a weak trend. Thus:

- Rising prices accompanied by falling volumes is a potentially bearish (negative) sign; and

- Falling prices accompanied by falling volumes is a potentially bullish (positive) sign.

There is however one caveat.

- It is generally observed that near the peak of an up trend a steep rise in a security's price is often accompanied by a huge 'burst' in volumes. This is potentially a bearish, and not a bullish, sign indicating that the big players are getting out of the stock by 'distributing' it to the smaller players.

- Conversely, near the bottom of a down trend, a steep fall in a security's price accompanied by any huge 'burst' in volumes is potentially a bullish and not a bearish sign and indicates that the big players are 'accumulating' the stock from the smaller players who are selling it.

Another point which should be kept in mind is that **a price break out — say, price breaking a resistance or a support line — when supported with higher than usual volumes is a good confirmation that the break out is a valid one.**

Thus, whenever a technical analyst sees a price pattern or a price break out, he will want to confirm it with corresponding volume expansion.

Finally, when volume is neither rising nor falling, the effect on price is neutral.

The Dow Theory

Way back in 1897, Charles Dow developed two indices to track the US stock markets. These are now called the Dow Jones Industrial Average (DJIA) and the Dow Jones Transportation Average. The Dow Jones Transportation Average originally consisted of railway companies which were a growth sector of that period.

The Dow Theory was the result of a compilation of the various articles Charles Dow wrote in the *Wall Street Journal.*

There are broadly six tenets of the Dow Theory. Let us review them and do so with relevant examples from the Indian context wherever relevant.

The Basic Tenets of Dow Theory

1. The Averages Discount Everything

Considered one of the basic assumptions of technical analysis, this is an important tenet. It suggests that the market price of a security is nothing but the combined impact of various factors affecting it, such as relevant news, information, the market players' reaction to these, including their emotional traits like hope, fear and greed, the financial power of select players', *et al.*

2. Market Movement Consists of Three Trends

The first among these is the **primary trend**. The primary trend indicates where the prices are 'generally' headed. It is the base trend and indicates whether the market is bullish or bearish.

For instance, movement of the Sensex from 2000 to 2003 was a primary down trend. During this period, and despite volatility, prices were generally going down. Conversely, the movement of the Sensex from 2003 to early 2007 (the time of writing this book) was a primary up trend, as prices moved generally higher, notwithstanding some intermittent corrections.

The next is the **secondary trend** which is nothing but the intermittent correction in prices in the opposite direction to the primary trend. Thus, when the primary trend is up intermittent downward corrections would constitute the secondary trend, and when the primary trend is down, intermittent up corrections would be a secondary trend.

The third type of trend is the **minor trend** comprising mainly of the day to day fluctuations. The Dow Theory holds that minor trends are insignificant since these are volatile and may be manipulated. One of the major corollaries of this is that the primary and secondary trends cannot be manipulated.

Chart 2.10 and Chart 2.11 of Nifty and Sensex depict primary and secondary trends.

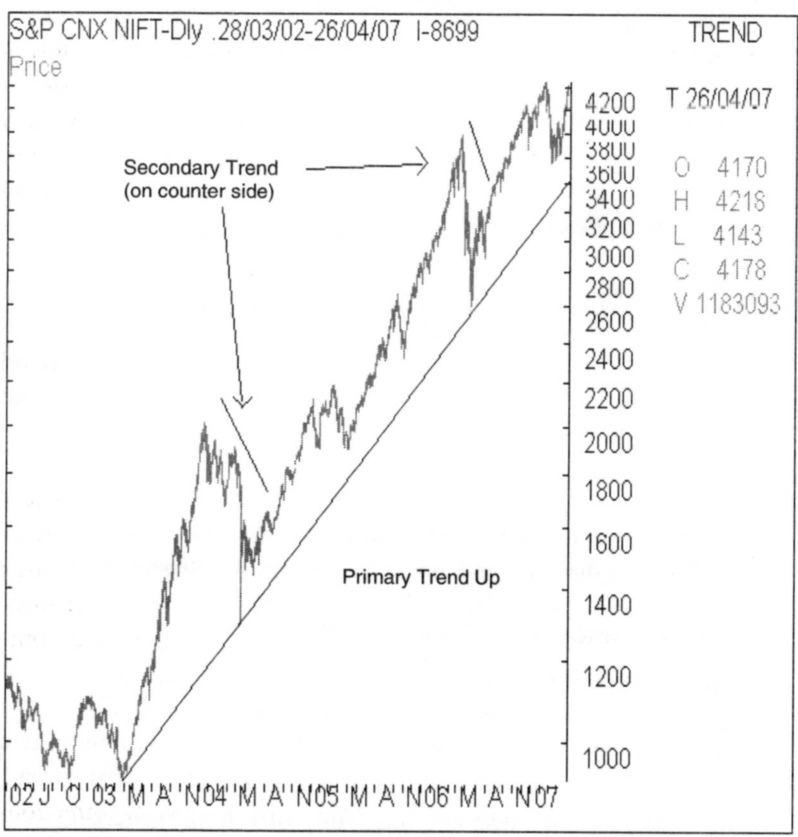

Chart 2.10: **Nifty's chart showing a primary up trend move with secondary downward trends running counter to the primary trend**

Chart 2.11: **Sensex Chart of 2000–2003 shows a primary down trend with secondary up trends running counter to the primary trend**

3. Primary Trends Have Three Phases

Dow recognized the relationship of the market's movement to the varying psyche of investors and accordingly identified three phases of the primary trend.

The first phase occurs near the beginning of a bullish market, when investment in stocks is considered taboo by the general public. In this phase it is the 'smart' investors who realize that prices have fallen much below their fundamentals and go in for what is popularly known as bottom fishing or bargain hunting. They have little competition since a majority of the investors have fled the scene. While the markets still appear to be in a bad shape, these smart investors realize that the worst is almost over and enter the market when prices are at near-bottom levels.

Thereafter comes the second phase when corporate results start showing signs of revival. Companies which had posted losses in previous quarter(s) either start showing a reduction in loss or hit break-even. It is in this phase that bigger investors, such as the institutions, FIIs, mutual funds and high net worth individuals (HNIs) who were earlier on the sidelines, slowly start pouring in money with each subsequent quarter of higher earnings.

Finally, and a few quarters after the second phase, comes the third phase of speculation and hyper speculation. It is in this phase that investors at large jump on to the bandwagon feeling that they have been missing out on all the action. The stock prices then spurt with higher velocity compared to that in the first two phases and one can see novices, young twenty-somethings, and even housewives talking of making money in the stock market. Day trading volumes rise dramatically accompanied by an equally dramatic rise in new fund offerings (NFOs) by mutual funds. All these could be treated as signs of a vibrantly speculative market.

In India, too, we've witnessed these phases, most recently in the current bull run since 2003. But this is not the only recent instance. There were similar phases during the Y2K software boom. Or, moving a little further in the past, one can recollect these phases during the phenomenal four-year bull run from 1988 to 1992. Sadly, both the bull runs of 1992 and 2000 ended with the unearthing of scams.

Similarly, bear markets too have three phases. The first phase of a bear market leads to a sell off from the market peak, with 'smart' investors exiting entirely realizing that the markets have gone much beyond their fundamentals. The second phase of selling occurs when corporate performance actually starts slowing down. The big players, such as the institutions, FIIs, mutual funds and HNIs start offloading their stock. The third phase is characterized by panic selling by the investors at large who would often have entered at the peak. They are forced to sell near the bottom, usually with big losses.

In India, a recent occurrence of these three phases of a bear market were seen during the crash which followed the Y2K software boom. Many investors who bought software stocks in the year 2000 ended up selling them at less than half the price in the following two years. There are examples galore!

4. The Averages (Indices) Must Confirm

Another tenet of the Dow Theory is that the two indices created by Dow, namely the Dow Jones Industrial Average and the Dow Jones Transportation Average, should confirm each other. Thus, a bullish trend in one average should also be confirmed by a similar bullish trend in the other. If one average is showing signs of trend reversal, the other one should, too.

5. Volumes Confirm the Trend

The Dow Theory holds that a primary trend, whether up or down, would be accompanied by volume expansion.

The volume expansion is indicative of larger market participation and confirms the strength of a trend. Thus, you would observe in Chart 2.12 that during 2002 and 2003 Nifty's volumes in the Index were relatively lower but as the markets started moving up, the volumes also expanded.

Chart 2.12: **This chart of Nifty highlights a bullish trend with rising volumes**

6. A Trend Remains Intact until it Gives a Definite 'Reversal'

The theory of trend analysis is based on the Dow Theory. As we noted earlier, a basic characteristic of a trend is the creation of either a higher high and higher low or a lower high and lower low formation. When these conditions are broken, a definitive trend reversal is said to have taken place.

Trend analysis is covered in detail in Chapter 3.

3

Price Patterns

'That history repeats itself, is a basic assumption of technical analysis.'

Why Price Patterns Occur — and Recur

Human nature shows repetitive tendencies in its display of emotions and behavior. More often than not people tend to repeat not only their positive behavior but also, more noticeably, their mistakes. There is an apt saying: 'What we learn from history is that we never learn from history'.

At its core, investing or trading is a game of psychology. Thus, what one witnesses in the seemingly erratic nature of price movements has at least as much to do with the emotions and behavior of investors and traders as with their rational thinking. The reaction of the various market players to news, data, rumor and hearsay tends to take on repetitive characteristics when viewed over a longer period of time.

The uncanny regularity of various market bubbles is an important illustration of this point. In the Indian context, we saw unprecedented excesses in certain old economy stocks till the year 1992. Once the bubble burst, the prices corrected themselves over the next eight years. Yes, that's how long it took for that particular irrationality to work itself out. But, then, behind the bubble of 1991-92 was the Harshad Mehta scam. Then came the technology bubble during 1999-2000 which carried prices of technology related 'new' economy stocks to dizzying heights. These again corrected themselves over the next three years, some of them by as much as 80% of their peak values.

The affected stocks may have been different but the basic investor behavior remained similar in both instances. In fact, if one goes back further in time many such similar or *deja vu* instances can be identified from all over the world.

Now if human behavior tends to repeat itself, the quantification of this behavior — in terms of price movements — would also tend to be repetitive.

This phenomenon is captured by technical analysts and is termed as price patterns or formations. Many academics and theorists have ridiculed the basic premise of recurring price patterns but it may be noted that such critics base their skepticism on the theoretical assumption of the existence of a perfect market place for securities — which is simply not the case in real life.

Price patterns are distinctive formations caused by changes in the forces of supply and demand which emerge when prices are plotted on a graph paper or, nowadays, charted using computer software.

These patterns have a meaning which can be interpreted in terms of probable future trend development. What then becomes important is the skill to identify these patterns on a price chart.

Types of Price Patterns

As a trader or investor, you are interested in figuring out whether the ongoing trend would continue, or whether it is likely to reverse. Accordingly, we will now consider two types of price pattern formations:

1. Continuation price patterns, and
2. Reversal price patterns.

Continuation Price Patterns

As we saw earlier, the formation of higher highs and higher lows indicates that an up trend is in progress while the formation of lower highs and lower lows indicates that the security or index is in a down trend. Continuation price patterns, on the other hand, suggest that prices are 'resting' for a while before resuming their move in the direction of the ongoing trend.

The following are some of the important continuation price patterns:

- Triangle price pattern;
- Rectangle price pattern;
- Bullish flag price pattern; and
- Bearish flag price pattern.

Triangle Price Pattern

How It is Formed

A triangle pattern is formed when, for a few days during an ongoing trend, prices form lower highs coupled with higher lows. The important point to note is that a triangle formation lasts for a relatively short period of time.

Interpretation

A triangle formation indicates that after a consistent rise or fall, as the case may be, traders and investors are pausing for a while to 'rest' and decide whether the price should go further in the earlier direction or not.

How to Trade a Triangle

For a short-term trader, the best strategy during a triangle formation is to exit the current trade (long or short, as the case may be) and wait for the price to break out from the triangle. Usually, the break out will be in the direction of the prevailing trend (Chart 3.01).

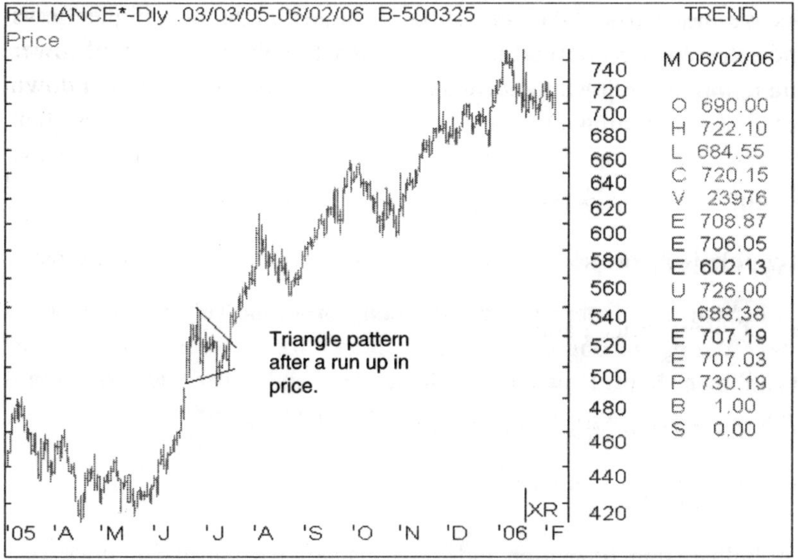

Chart 3.01: **This chart of Reliance Industries shows a triangle continuation price pattern. You would observe that the price run was steep from ₹ 430 levels to ₹ 540 levels, after which the price 'rested' in the triangle before resuming its up move.**

Rectangle Price Pattern

How It is Formed

A rectangle price pattern is formed when, for a few days during an ongoing trend, prices tend to form almost equal highs coupled with almost equal lows. Again, as in the case of all continuation patterns, this formation lasts for a relatively short period of time.

Interpretation

A rectangle formation indicates that after a consistent rise or fall, as the case may be, the market is pausing to decide whether the price should go further in the ongoing direction or not.

How to Trade a Rectangle

Again, the best strategy during a rectangle formation is to exit the current trade (long or short, as the case may be) and wait for the price to break out from the rectangle. Usually the break out will be in the direction of the prevailing trend. Chart 3.02 depicts this pattern in the case of gold futures

Bullish Flag Price Pattern

How It is Formed

A bullish flag pattern is formed when, for a relatively few number of days during an ongoing up trend, prices form lower highs coupled with lower lows. However, the lower high and lower low formation is not large enough to suggest a reversal of the up trend.

Interpretation

A bullish flag formation indicates that after a consistent price rise, certain sections of the market are putting selling pressure on the price — hence the lower low formations — but are unsuccessful in convincing a majority of the players of a change in trend.

Chart 3.02: **A rectangular continuation price pattern in an ongoing up move in gold futures. This sort of a pattern is many a time referred to by analysts as a 'sideways' correction.**

How to Trade Bullish Flags

Again, the best strategy during a bullish flag formation is to exit the current trade and wait for a break out of prices beyond the most recent high. Usually the break out will be in the up direction. Chart 3.03 depicts a bullish flag pattern.

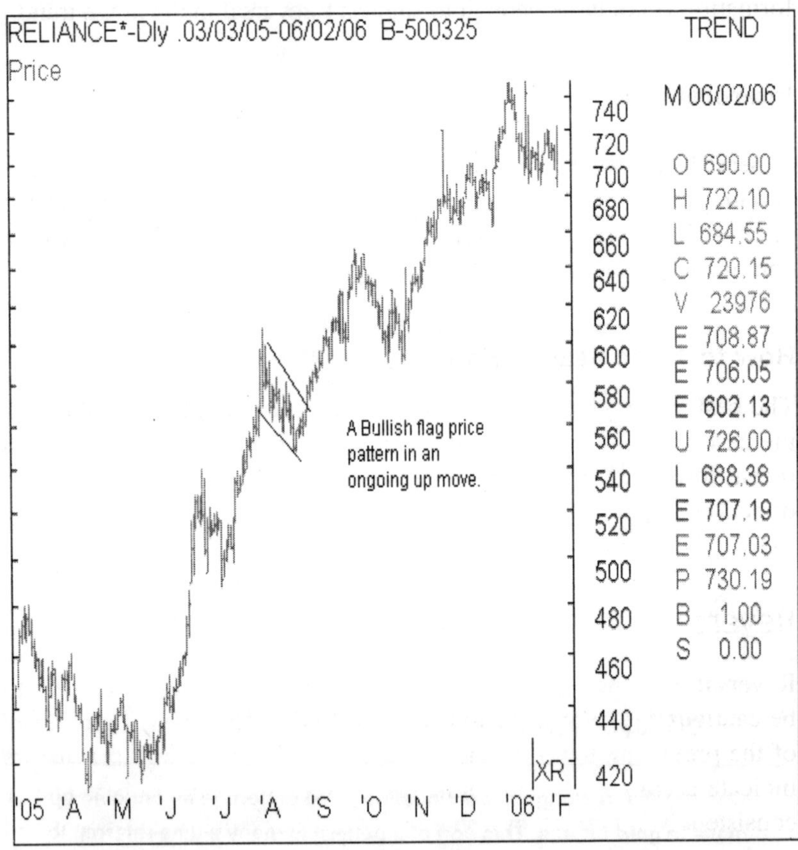

Chart 3.03: **A bullish flag pattern in the chart of Reliance Industries. You can observe that during the formation of the flag, the prices tried to make a lower high and lower low formation, but the lower lows were not significant enough to suggest a reversal.**

Bearish Flag Price Pattern

How It is Formed

This is a price formation which occurs during an ongoing down trend, when for a relatively short period, prices tend to form higher highs coupled with higher lows. However, the higher high and higher low formation is not large enough to suggest a reversal in the down trend.

Interpretation

A bearish flag formation indicates that after a consistent fall in price, certain sections of the market are creating buying pressure on the price — hence the higher high formations — but are not successful in convincing the other players of a change in trend.

How to Trade Bearish Flags

The best strategy, again, is to exit the current trade (long or short, as the case may be) and wait for a break out of prices beyond the most recent low. Usually, the break out will be in the original downward direction

Reversal Price Patterns

Reversal price patterns are formations which warn market players to be cautious as the price action is suggestive of an impending reversal of the prevailing trend. In most cases, price formations of this nature indicate a climax-like situation. Thus, excessive panic selling after a consistent bear market, or a sharp rally in stocks after a consistent bull market could be warning signs from the market for traders and investors to become cautious and remain on high alert. The following price formations indicate a reversal of trend:

- Double top formation;
- Double bottom formation;

- Triple top and bottom formations;
- Head and shoulders price formations;
- Inverse head and shoulders price formations;
- Rounding top reversal; and
- Rounding bottom reversal.

Double Top Formation

How It is Formed

A double top price pattern forms, usually at the end of a consistent rise in prices, when the price re-tests a previous high but is unable to go any higher since it finds more sellers than buyers at the previous high level and is thus unable to form a higher high.

Interpretation

A double top formation usually occurs at the end of a long up trend. The security's failure to break above the previous high price level and its subsequent move downward are suggestive that a new high is not made and therefore the basic premise of an up trend, namely the formation of higher highs and higher lows, is not satisfied. This fact cautions investors and traders that a reversal may now be due. .

How to Trade a Double Top

Once the price re-tests a previous high and then starts retracing back lower, a trader can sell, or short sell, with a stop loss* kept just above the previous equal high recently reached. A trader may expect the price to fall at least to the most recent low price level, or even further below that as follows:

Target price = Previous low – (Previous high – Previous low)

---

* The concept and use of stop loss is briefly explained on page 62.

Thus, if the previous high of a scrip was say, ₹ 110, its most recent low ₹ 95, and it re-tests ₹ 110 but starts falling back again, the minimum target would be ₹ 95 (previous low), and optimistic down target would be ₹ 80 [(i.e. 95 – (110–95)].

Chart 3.04 illustrates a double top formation in the case of Siemens India. You will observe that we have ignored the one-day spike in prices above ₹ 1,400 as that price move could be invalid, i.e. not representative of the buying interest. The scrip faced resistance at ₹ 1,300+ levels for the second time and then started falling lower.

Chart 3.04: **Siemens India's chart showing a double top formation**

The immediate target would be the most recent previous low, which is at ₹ 760 (support line indicated in the chart). A break below this support line of ₹ 760 would then suggest a reversal of the entire up trend.

Double Bottom Formation

How It is Formed

A double bottom is formed, usually at the end of a consistent fall in prices, when the price of a security or index re-tests the previous low made by it but finds more buyers than sellers at that previous low price level, in the process forming an equal low or bottom on the chart.

Interpretation

A double bottom formation usually occurs at the end of a long down trend. The security's failure to break below the previous low price level, and its subsequent move upward, suggest that a new low has not been made and, therefore, the basic premise of a down trend, namely lower highs and lower lows, is not satisfied. This fact should alert investors and traders that a reversal in the prevailing down trend may now be due.

How to Trade a Double Bottom

Once the price re-tests a previous low and then starts retracing higher without making a lower low, a trader / investor can buy with a stop loss kept just below the equal low price recently reached. A trader may expect the price to rise at least to the immediate previous high price level and, optimistically, even higher as follows:

Target price = Previous high + (Previous high — Previous low)

Let us suppose the previous low of a scrip was say, ₹ 75 and its most recent high ₹ 100. If the price re-tests ₹ 75 but starts rising again without going any lower, the minimum target would be ₹ 100 (previous high), and the optimistic up target ₹ 125 [i.e., 100 + (100–75)].

Chart 3.05 of Wipro Ltd. shows an example of a double bottom formation. You will observe that after reaching the upper resistance line (the first target after the double bottom was formed) the scrip gave a break out of the resistance suggesting a reversal of the ongoing down trend. Please see marking's on the chart.

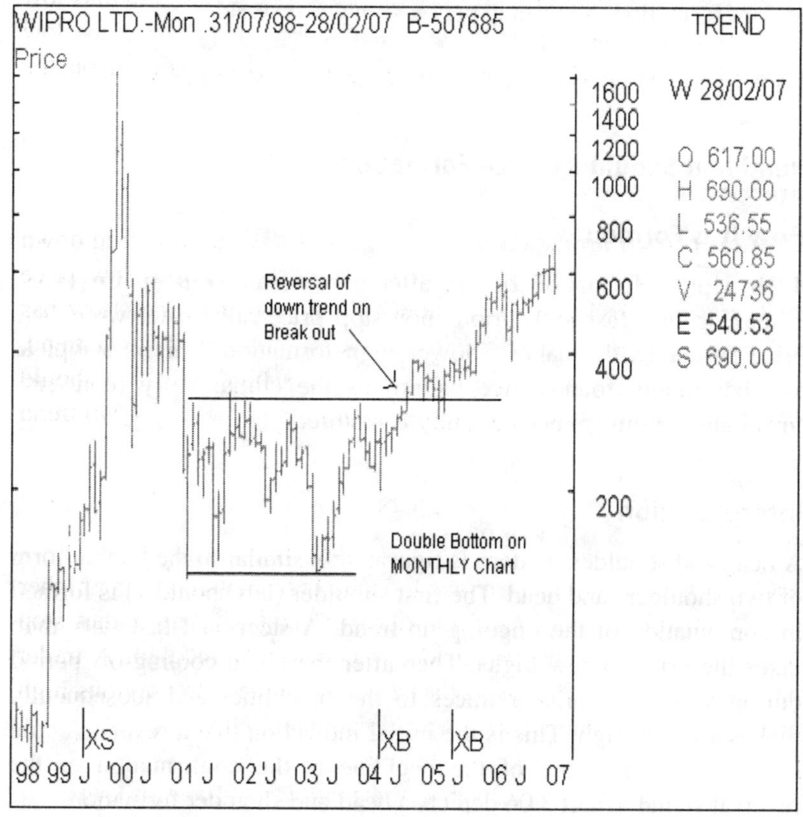

Chart 3.05: **Wipro Ltd. monthly chart indicating a double bottom formation**

Triple Top and Bottom Formations

While the basic reasons for these price patterns and the strategy for trading them remains similar to double top or double bottom formations, the triple bottom formation indicates prices have thrice found support at a particular price level. Conversely, a triple top formation indicates that prices have thrice found resistance at a particular price level.

Thus, when a security finally confirms a reversal from a triple top or bottom formation, one can expect a stronger reversal.

Triple top and bottom price formations are relatively rare.

Head and Shoulders Price Formation

How It is Formed

Such a price formation occurs after a consistent run up in prices, climaxing in a fast and furious non-stop price rally, after which the price subsequently makes a lower high formation. This is a typical and commonly found price pattern as the climax rally represents 'irrational' optimism before sanity is restored

Interpretation

A head and shoulders pattern is figuratively similar to the human form of two shoulders and head. The first shoulder (left shoulder) is formed in continuation of the ongoing up trend. A steep and fast rally then takes the price to new highs. Thereafter there is a cooling-off period during which the price retraces to the 'neckline' and subsequently makes a lower high. This is the initial indication that a reversal could be due. The breaking of the neckline is the confirmation of the reversal signal. Chart 3.06 depicts a head and shoulder formation.

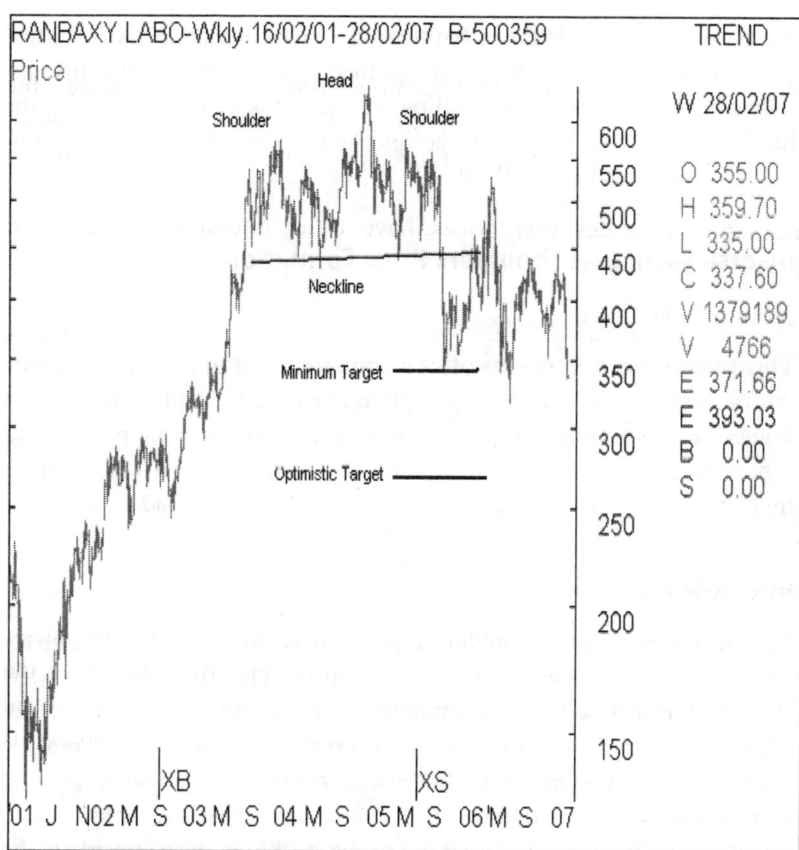

Chart 3.06: **Weekly chart of Ranbaxy Laboratories showing a head and shoulders pattern. You will observe that on the break out of the neckline support line, the price fell to the first target by as much as the distance from the right shoulder to the neckline (₹ 100). The possible target too is indicated which is near the ₹ 260-270 levels, being the distance between the head and the neckline from the neckline break out.**

How to Trade the Head and Shoulders Formation

Once the price breaks below the neckline, a short position can be initiated with a stop loss just above the right shoulder (the recent lower high formed). A trader can then expect the price to fall at least by as much as the distance between the right shoulder and neckline and, possibly, even lower by a magnitude of which equals the distance between the head and the neckline. Usually, the distance between the head and neckline is quite large and hence a reversal following this pattern leads to a huge sell off.

Inverse Head and Shoulders Price Formation

How It is Formed

This price formation occurs after a consistent fall in prices, climaxing with a fast and furious non-stop price crash and, finally, ending in a higher low formation. This is a typical price pattern as the panic crash represents 'extreme' human pessimism ('end of the world') before investors realize that things may not really be quite as bad.

Interpretation

An inverse head and shoulders formation is, figuratively, the mirror image of a head and shoulders formation. The first shoulder (left shoulder) is formed in continuation with the ongoing down trend. Then a steep and fast crash takes the price to a new low. Thereafter, there is some cooling off and prices retrace to the neckline and subsequently make a higher low. This is an initial indication that a reversal may be due. The breaking of the neckline on the upside is the confirmation of the reversal signal.

How to Trade an Inverse Head and Shoulders Pattern

Once the price breaks out above the neckline, long positions can be initiated with a stop loss just below the right shoulder (the most recent higher low formed). A trader can expect the price to rise by at least the magnitude of the distance between the right shoulder and neckline and, optimistically, even higher equal to the magnitude of the distance between the head and the neckline. Usually the distance between the head and neckline is quite large and hence a reversal after this pattern leads to a huge rally. Chart 3.07 illustrates an inverse head and shoulders formation.

Chart 3.07: **Japanese Nikkei index showing an inverse head and shoulders reversal pattern. You will observe that the monthly chart of the Japanese Nikkei Index indicated in mid-2005 that the multi-year down trend was reversing. You will also observe that the optimistic target (index level of 17,000) too was reached in mid-2006.**

Rounding Top Reversal

How It is Formed

This price formation occurs at the later stage of the price rally when, after a consistent rise, prices fail to make significant highs despite strong market interest as indicated by volumes. Thus the situation becomes one of high volumes of trading but without any marked increase in price. During the subsequent days of a rounding top, prices make lows, but not significant new lows. A graphical view of such a situation crystallizes on the price chart as a 'rounding' pattern.

Interpretation

The most important aspect which I have observed in the case of a rounding top pattern is that the high volumes coupled with insignificant price movement is suggestive of a slow distribution taking place. Effectively, the bigger 'smart' players are slowly selling off, or 'distributing', their holdings to the mass of individual investors. They are doing so slowly in order that they may be able to offload their entire holdings without leading to a significant price fall. By keeping the prices from falling too much, they can exit their positions more profitably. Another important observation is that price tends towards the levels where the rounding pattern initially started.

How to Trade a Rounding Top

Usually a rounding top formation takes some days to develop during which the price tends to move in a roughly defined range. Since it is a rounding top formation, a trader can wait for the low of the range to be broken before initiating a short sell position, and investors may then exit their long (buy) positions. The trader can keep a stop loss just above the high of the range and hold his short position for a down target near the starting point of the pattern as indicated in Chart 3.08.

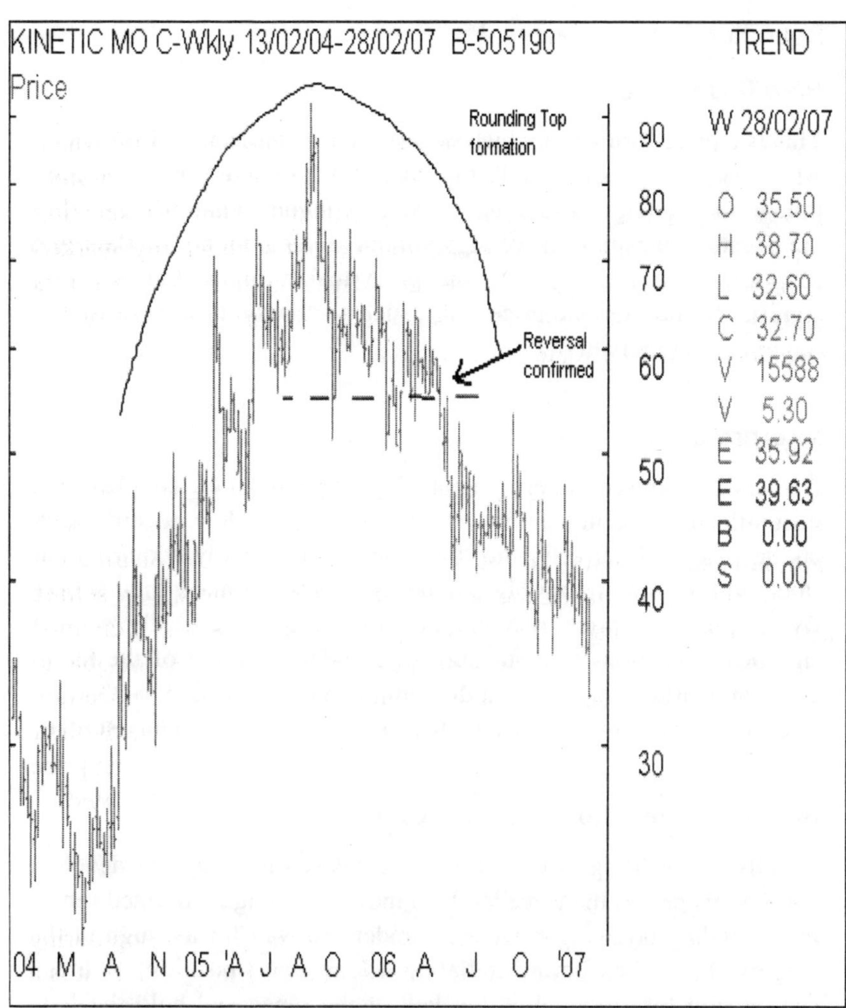

Chart 3.08: **Kinetic Motor Company's weekly chart showing a rounding top formation. After consolidation, the price started making equal lows and slightly lower lows, suggesting a pressure on prices. The break below this 'support' level leads to further aggressive selling.**

Rounding Bottom Reversal

How It is Formed

This is a price formation which occurs after a consistent fall in prices. At the later stages of the fall, the price fails to make significant lows though the trading interest measured by volumes remains high. Thus the situation becomes one of high volume trading but no 'marked' fall in price. With passing days the price makes highs, but not very significant ones. On the price chart, such a situation unveils itself as a rounding bottom pattern.

Interpretation

A rounding bottom pattern, signaled by high volumes coupled with insignificant price movement, is suggestive of a slow accumulation taking place. Effectively, the 'big' players are slowly acquiring the stock without attempting big purchases in order to mask their action. By keeping the price rise gradual, they can more easily acquire significant positions without attracting undue attention of the larger body of market players. Another important observation is that the price tends towards levels where the rounding pattern actually started.

How to Trade a Rounding Bottom

Usually, a rounding bottom formation takes some days to develop. During this period the price tends to move in a roughly defined range. In a rounding bottom formation, a trader can wait for the high of the range to be broken before initiating a long (buy) position. You can keep a stop loss just below the low of the range and hold the long position for an upper target near the starting point of the pattern as indicated in Chart 3.09.

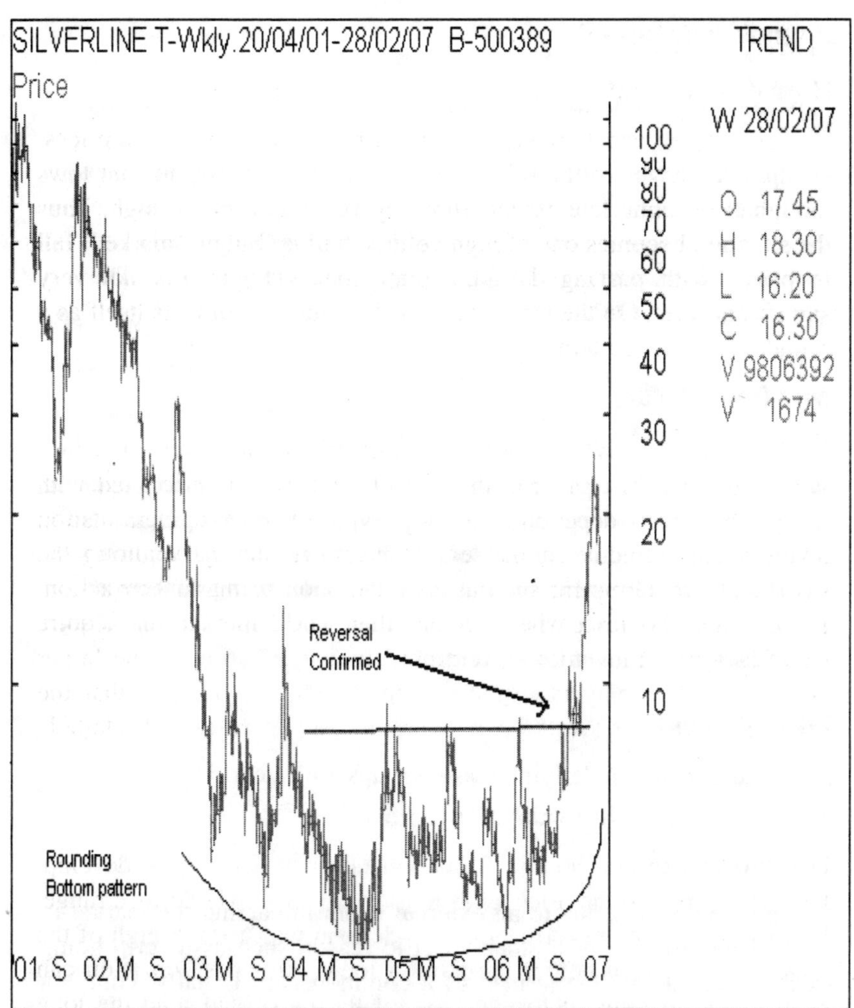

Chart 3.09: **Weekly chart of Silverline Technologies. After consolidation, the price started making equal highs and slightly higher highs, suggesting a demand for the stock. The break above this 'resistance' level leads to further aggressive buying.**

Briefly: Gaps

Gaps are often found in price charts when the markets are volatile.

A gap occurs when the opening price of a security (or an index) is significantly higher, or lower, than its immediate previous closing price. Thus, if say a security closes at ₹ 125 on Monday and opens on Tuesday at a price of, say ₹ 132, we say that a gap is created. The gap size in this case is ₹ 7.

Why Gaps Occur

Gaps occur mainly because of some significant developments happening after the closing of the market. This leads to prices opening higher or lower depending on the type of development. Such developments could be announcement of results after market hours, or a corporate development such as an acquisition being announced, or in the Indian context, when US or other world markets have seen significant price movements overnight.

Types of Gaps

Depending on the underlying reasons, gaps are categorized as:

Common Gaps

When a gap occurs due to an external event impacting the market in general, or because of a stock-specific reason such as a scrip going ex-dividend, it may be termed as a common gap. Usually, common gaps tend to get 'filled in' by the price action of the next few days.

Break Out Gaps

When a particular security's price is hovering near an important support or resistance line, or has been range-bound for some time, the support / resistance lines may be broken with prices opening in gaps above or below the support or resistance level. Chart 3.10. illustrates a break out gap.

Exhaustion Gaps

After an ongoing rally or an ongoing fall, many a time markets open in gaps in the direction of the price move, only to reverse direction in the next few days. In fact, such gaps at the 'extremes' are suggestive of the market's 'tiredness' and can mean a 'distribution' by bigger players. Chart 3.10 shows an exhaustion gap in the case of Ranbaxy during the first few days of May 2006. In the following days, the prices did not even go above the high of the 'gap day'. Usually, there will be higher volume when exhaustion gaps are created.

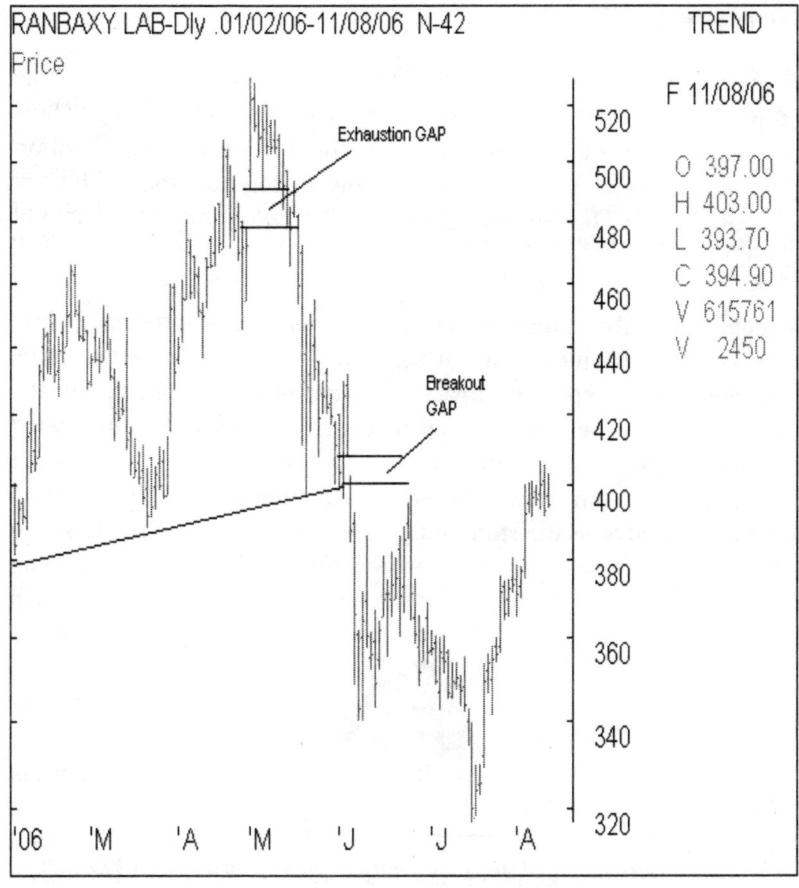

Chart 3.10: **Example of a break out gap and an exhaustion gap.**

Runaway Gaps

These are rare gaps created usually near the peak, or a low, after prices have been consolidating for some time. The gap then created (mostly based on stock-specific news) does not get filled in and new and more aggressive buying (or selling, as the case may be) occurs despite the higher (or lower, as the case may be) prices. In fact, this new buying (or selling) at a later stage develops into a trend. Which is why such gaps are termed as 'runaway' gaps.

Stop Loss*

Most traders are familiar with the term stop loss. It literally means 'stopping your loss' in case your analysis proves to be wrong. Thus, stop loss is a price level where a trader would exit his trading position if the market were to against him. Many traders use some arbitrary stop loss, say 2% below buying price or ₹ 5 below buying price, and so on.

A technical analyst however will use the term more prudently. Any trade — a buy position or a sell position — is based on certain price behavior and its expected impact on future price movement. But the trader must also be alert enough to exit his trade if the anticipated movement does not materialize due to, say, a change in market condition or on some new information affecting price. This exit price level is referred to as the stop loss.

---

* For a full understanding of stop losses, please see *Stop Orders — A Practical Guide to Using Stop Orders for Traders and Investors* (Vision Books, New Delhi, www.visionbooksindia.com)

4

Moving Averages

'If not the Gods, put the odds on your side!'

Meaning of a Moving Average

Statistically speaking, a simple average is defined as the summation of the values of the various observations, divided by the number of observations. Thus:

$$\text{Simple average} = \frac{\text{Sum of values of n observations}}{\text{n}}$$

Thus if we have, say, 20 days of price data, the sum of the prices of these twenty days divided by 20 will give us the simple average price.

Now, on the 21st day we have another price data. In order to compute afresh the 20-day average price, we need to exclude the 1st day's price and include in its place the price of the 21st day.

Example 4.1

For the purpose of understanding please refer to the following hypothetical price data and the corresponding graph depicting the 5-day moving average:

Price	5-Day Moving Average
100.00	
98.50	
99.00	
101.00	
102.00	100.10
102.00	100.50
103.00	101.40
104.50	102.50
106.00	103.50
108.00	104.70
106.50	105.60
108.50	106.70

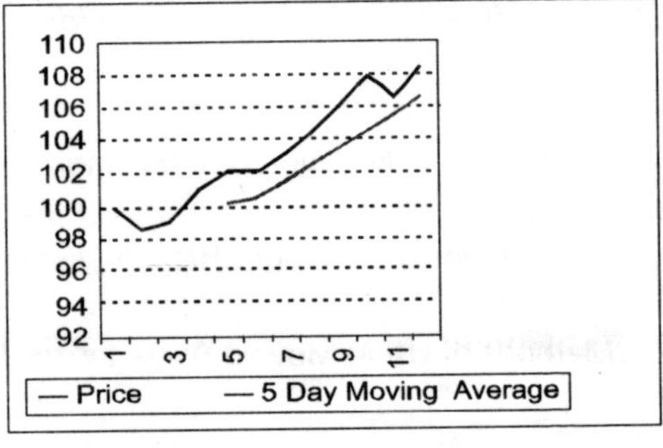

You would observe from this that since we are calculating a 5-day moving average, the first moving average value appears on the fifth day. This first value of the moving average is the simple average of the prices of the first five days and the value works out to ₹ 100.10. On the subsequent day, i.e. the sixth day, the first day's price (₹ 100) is excluded and the sixth day's (₹ 102) is added in its place and the value of the average then works out to ₹ 100.50.

To get familiar with the computation, you may try the above manually.

Similarly, in order to compute average price of 20 days on the 22nd day, we need to exclude the 1st and 2nd day's prices and include the 21st and 22nd days' prices. And so on, as new data comes in, we 'move' one day such that the most recent data is included.

Accordingly you would observe that when we want to compute a 20-day moving average, we are effectively considering the price data of the most recent 20 days.

Similarly, therefore, if one wants to compute, say, the moving average of 50 days, price data of the most recent 50 days will be averaged, the process of inclusion of new data and exclusion of old data remaining the same as explained above.

Chart 4.01 depicts the movement of the Sensex along with its 34-day moving average (34 DMA). You would observe that moving average is 'superimposed' on the price chart.

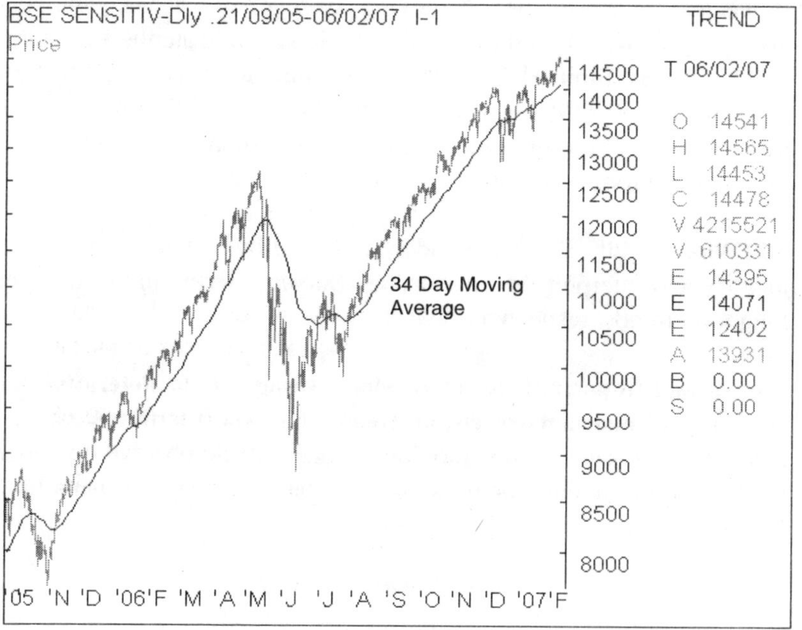

Chart 4.01: **Sensex with its 34-day moving average (DMA)**

Also, considering the computation process of a moving average, it is obvious that the 5-day moving average will reflect more recent price data than would a 50-day moving average.

How Moving Averages Help in Studying Price Behavior

While a moving average is essentially a derivation from the price data, it is very useful in understanding the behavior of prices.

One important use of moving averages is that they can help in identifying the ongoing trend of prices. Since any moving average has a tendency of smoothening out the seemingly erratic daily price fluctuations, it affords a clearer picture of the underlying trend of prices.

If we take a shorter period moving average, say a 5-day moving average (usually referred to as 5 DMA), it will indicate the short term trend of prices. Similarly, if we take a medium term period such as 30 days, then a 30 DMA will tell us the direction of the intermediate trend. Likewise, a long term moving average such as 200 DMA will highlight the long-term, or primary, trend of prices.

50 DMA and 200 DMA are widely followed by technical analysts to identify and interpret the intermediate (medium term) and primary or long term trends, respectively.

The second important use of moving averages is to determine the support and resistance levels, or areas. Thus, short term traders who are following, say, a 5–day moving average, would observe that price tends to find support, or resistance as the case may be, near its 5 DMA value.

Similarly, long term investors using price charts for decision making, will observe that prices tend to find support, or face resistance, near their 200 DMA.

Since they can also help identify a change in trend, **the third important use of a moving average is that it actually helps a trader or investor to enter or exit a trade**. Details of the methods of using this tool are given in the ensuing section.

Using Moving Averages for Trading and Investing

Since moving averages can tell us when a trend has changed direction, they are the bases of many trend-following trading methods.

In a trending market, i.e. when markets are in a clear up trend or down trend, moving average based trades will generate highly profitable results, and do so with relative safety.

As a corollary, moving average based trades will not be profitable in non-trending markets, i.e. when markets are moving sideways.

It is important to point out here that the trend reversal price patterns we studied earlier in Chapter 3 are the key for identifying reversals. Moving averages, on the other hand, are additional evidence of a trend change and may be treated as supportive evidence.

Method 1: Price Crossing Above or Below a Moving Average

A simple way of using the moving average is to buy when the price rises above its defined period's moving average, and sell when it falls below the moving average.

It is obvious that shorter the moving average period, the more the prices will have a tendency to fluctuate, or oscillate, above and below it. Hence, it is advisable for traders and investors to take a medium term period moving average for this purpose.

Medium term traders may take a period of more than 20 days while investors may prefer a period of 50 days or more.

My observation has been that the medium term trend of the Sensex (BSE 30 Index) is adequately captured by its 34-day moving average. This means that the medium term — or, intermediate — trend of the Sensex is bullish (positive) so long as the Sensex remains above its 34-day moving average, and bearish (weak) when it remains below its 34-day moving average (Chart 4.01).

You may want to validate this observation.

Practical Hint

Enter the trade the day after the Sensex breaks out beyond its 34-DMA and goes beyond the high, or low as the case may be, of the signal day. Thus:

- If a buy signal is generated today the strategy should be to buy tomorrow if today's high is surpassed.

- Similarly, if a sell signal is generated today, then the strategy would be to sell tomorrow if today's low is broken.

This sort of 'filtering' will greatly reduce the number of 'false signals', which such a method may generate.

Thus, let's suppose you get a buy signal today as prices go above the defined period's moving average. Now using the filtering technique, you would actually buy tomorrow only if today's high is surpassed. This will give you an idea whether the market is 'really comfortable' with the new higher prices and whether there is a sustainable buying momentum.

Conversely, let's say you get a sell signal today as prices go below the defined period's moving average. Using the filtering technique, you would actually sell tomorrow and that too only if today's low is broken. This will give you an idea whether the market is really comfortable with the new lower prices, and whether there really is a sustained selling pressure.

Method 2: Trading the Slope of the Moving Average

Trading the slope method tries to overcome one of the drawbacks of the moving average tool — namely, that it does not lead to profitable deals in non-trending markets.

The slope, or steepness, of a moving average line can suggest whether the price is trending or simply moving sideways. If the moving average line is going up steeply, it indicates a strong up trend while if it is falling steeply it suggests a strong down trend. In such cases, trades in the direction of the moving average line will be profitable.

But if the moving average line is turning flat, i.e. growing more horizontal rather than sloping steeply upward or downwards, it indicates a range bound or non-trending price movement and tells the trader not to trade for the time being.

A major advantage of such a method is that it keeps you in the trend for a longer time. Chart 4.02 of Hindustan Petroleum (HPCL) depicts the use of this method.

Method 3: The Two Moving Average Crossover Method

So far we have considered trading signals when the price crosses over the moving average. Most technical analysts, however, typically use more than one moving average on the price charts. Usually, two moving averages are used and their crossover is considered as a signal for entering or exiting a trade.

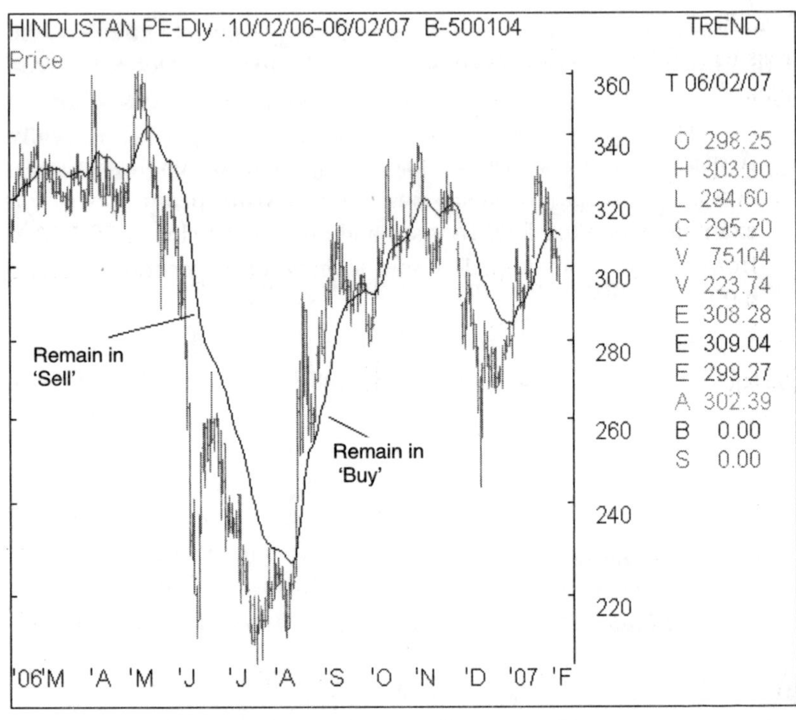

Chart 4.02: **How to use the slope of a moving average**

One of the two moving averages is a shorter period moving average and the other a longer period one. Thus you may decide to use, say, 5 DMA as the short period moving average and 20 DMA as the longer period moving average. Alternatively, if your time frame for trading or investing is longer, you may decide to use 50 DMA as the short period moving average and 200 DMA as the longer period moving average.

How Trading Signals are Generated Using the Crossover Method

Since one of the moving averages selected is of a shorter term and the other one of a longer term, it is obvious that the shorter term moving average will change faster and the longer term moving average will be slower to change.

Periodically, the values of these two moving averages will intersect or cross each other. The intersection, or crossing over, is considered as a signal for entering or exiting a trade:

- **A buy signal is generated when the short term moving average crosses the longer term moving average from below.** Thus, for example, when the 5 DMA rises and crosses the slower 20 DMA from below, a buy signal is said to have been generated (Chart 4.03).

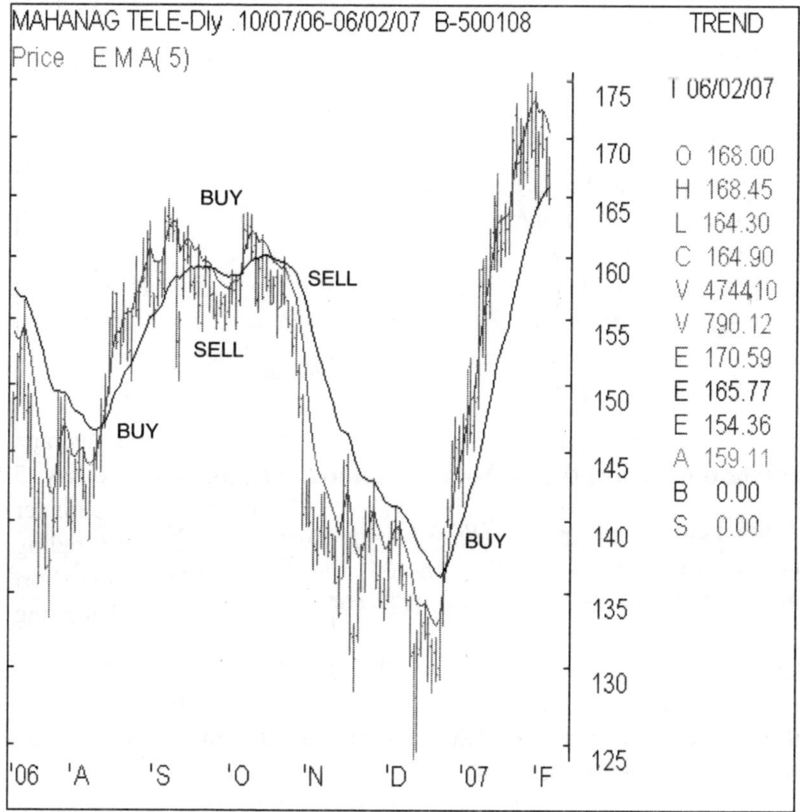

Chart 4.03: **MTNL's chart showing the buy and sell signals generated by the two moving average crossover system**

- Conversely, a sell signal is generated when the short term moving average crosses the longer term moving average from above. Thus, when the 5 DMA drops and crosses the slower 20 DMA from above, a sell signal is said to have been generated (Chart 4.03).

The author's observation is that a crossover of 5 DMA and 20 DMA gives profitable signals on the daily charts for medium term trading, especially for the Sensex (BSE 30 Index) and for its component companies (the 30 stocks representing the Sensex).

The reader may want to validate the above observation.

Practical Hint

Enter the trade on break out of the high, or low as the case may be, on the day after the crossover signal is generated.

As explained in Method 1 earlier, this sort of filtering is useful in reducing the number of false signals. Such filtering helps to test whether the market is really comfortable with the new prices after the signal has been generated.

Method 4: Using the 'Magnetic' Characteristic of 200 DMA

A practical use of the 200 DMA for a long term investor is provided by the direction of the moving average. When the 200 DMA is moving upward, the overall sentiment is bullish, and *vice versa*.

Experience highlights a noteworthy point that the 200 DMA effectively acts as a magnet for the stock price. When the price moves too far away from the 200 DMA, it 'attracts' the price back towards itself, as if asking for a re-test of the 200 DMA line.

Thus, when the trend is bullish, prices will sometimes roam far above the 200 DMA line, which then attracts them back closer towards itself. Thus, in such a case, the price then tends to fall in a corrective move towards the 200 DMA and come closer to it — as if the market is wondering about its bullish mood.

Conversely, when the trend is bearish, prices have a tendency to sometimes stray much below the 200 DMA, which then attracts them back towards itself. Thus, the prices tend to rise in a corrective pullback move towards the 200 DMA — as though the market is deciding whether to continue with its bearish mood.

This is a typical characteristic of price behavior *vis-a-vis* the 200 DMA on various securities across different markets.

Let's now see some examples of this phenomenon.

In Charts 4.04, 4.05 and 4.06, you can see this tango of the price and its 200 DMA: each time the price goes too far from the DMA, it tends to move back towards it — until the trend reverts.

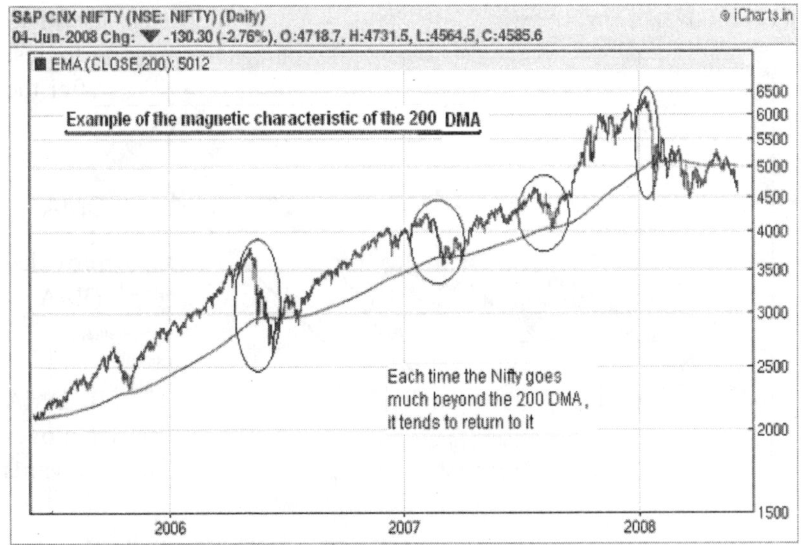

Chart 4.04: **Example of the 'magnetic' characteristic of the 200 DMA — each time the Nifty goes much beyond the 200 DMA, it tends to return to it**

Chart 4.05: **The 'magnetic' characteristic of the 200 DMA in bullish and bearish markets in Infosys**

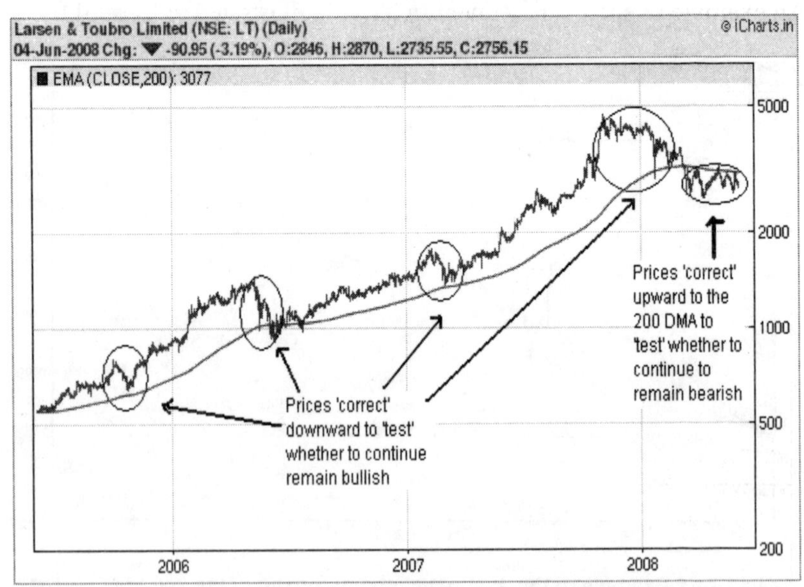

Chart 4.06: **The 'magnetic' characteristic of the 200 DMA in the chart of Larsen and Toubro**

How to use 200 DMA's Magnetic Characteristic for Short Term and Medium Term Trading

The characteristic of the 200 DMA attracting the price to it gives the medium term trader — one with a trading horizon of 3 to 4 weeks — an opportunity to trade the security towards the 200 DMA.

For this you may use technical indicators, such as the divergence on the RSI or a crossover of the medium term moving averages, e.g. 5 DMA and 21 DMA, to provide the required clue as to when the price is likely to move towards its 200 DMA.

Thus, for instance, if the price is much below the 200 DMA and then one observes a buy signal generated by a crossover of the medium term moving averages, (for example 5 EMA crossover of 21 EMA — please see Chart 4.07) it becomes more likely that the price will get attracted towards the 200 DMA.

An example of such a movement in Nifty is illustrated in Chart 4.07.

Chart 4.07: **Sell and buy signals generated by DMA crossover offer trading opportunities explaining the magnetic characteristic of the 200 DMA**

Method 5: Using 'n' Period High or Low Moving Averages

One of the major advantages of moving averages is that the technical trader can use them in many different ways. In practice, many market technicians do actually adjust moving averages to suit their own style, method and techniques.

Thus, another variation of using moving averages is to compute the moving average based only on either the 'highs' or the 'lows' of last 'n' periods, instead of the usual method of computing a moving average using the closing prices of the previous 'n' periods.

The modified moving average can be used in two ways.

1. Assume in the first instance that we are computing the moving average. If the price is above the moving average based on price highs, we can assume a strong up trend.

   Conversely, If the price is below the moving average based on the lows, we can assume a strong down trend.

2. The second method of using the moving averages of the highs or the lows is as follows:

   When we superimpose on the chart the moving average of the highs during an ongoing down move, prices have a tendency to 'test' the moving averages in corrective rises, i.e. pullback rallies.

   Conversely, when we superimpose on the chart the moving average of the lows, during an ongoing up move, prices have a tendency to 'test' the moving averages in corrective falls.

These 'tests' of moving average gives opportunity to re-enter trade in direction of the trend.

The use of both the above techniques is explained with the help of examples illustrated in Charts 4.08 and 4.09.

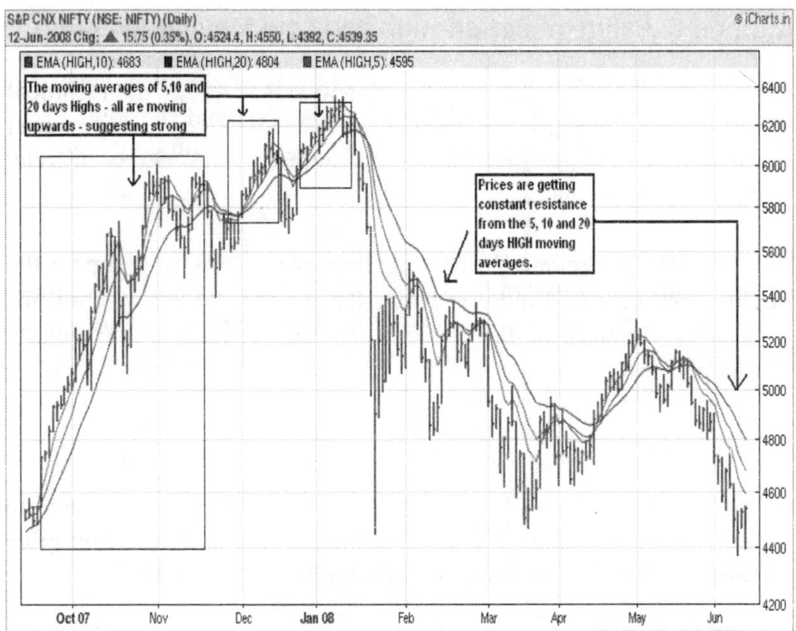

Chart 4.08: **During down trend prices 'test' the 5, 10 and 20 days moving averages of the Highs and then resume the earlier trend**

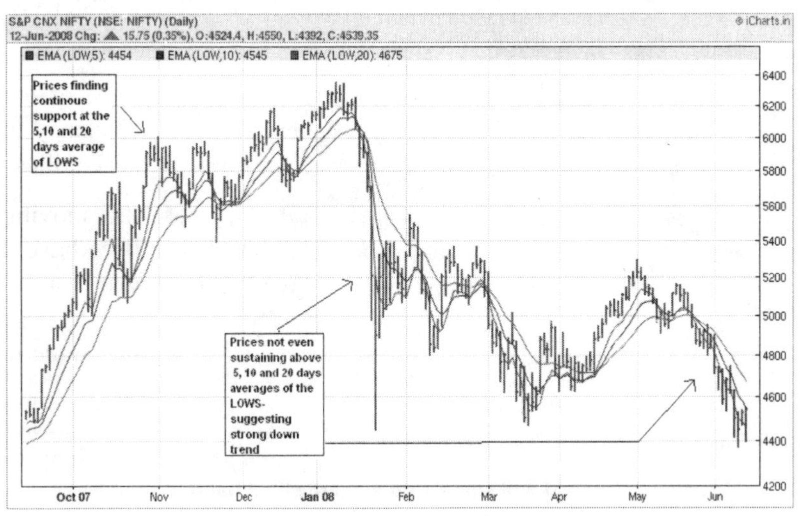

Chart 4.09: **During up trend prices 'test' the 5, 10 and 20 days moving averages of the Lows and then resume the earlier trend**

Method 6: Using 'n' Period High and Low Moving Averages

Another method of using moving averages is to simultaneously plot the moving average of the highs of 'n' periods and the lows of 'n' periods. The band thus formed would give us a 'filtered' entry, or exit, from a trade.

For instance, in Chart 4.10, we have considered the moving averages of the highs and lows of 20 days. Now, whenever the price closes below the 20-day moving average of the lows, it's a signal to sell and whenever the price closes above the 20-day high moving average of the highs, it is a signal to buy.

One advantage of this method of using the moving averages is that during periods of price stagnation, namely during non-trending market periods, there will be no signal and hence the overall number of trades will be fewer. This is a good thing in a sideways market.

Chart 4.10: **Buy and sell signals on a chart with a band formed by 20-period moving average of highs and lows which suggests good entry and exits into trades but does not give targets**

The basic idea of this method of using moving averages is to catch the trend while using filtering based on the moving average itself.

Which Type of Moving Average to Use

Moving averages may be of different types depending on how they are computed. The most common ones are:

- Simple moving average (SMA);
- Exponential moving average (EMA); and
- Weighted moving average (WMA).

Example 4.1 at the start of this chapter is based on a simple moving average. However, most price charting software has the facility of plotting all three types of moving averages. **The author's experience has been that exponential moving averages give better results**, since they smoothen the simple averages.

Bollinger Bands

Developed by John Bollinger, Bollinger bands attempt to capture the volatility of a security's price movements, using a moving average as the base.

Bollinger bands consist of three lines. One is a pre-defined moving average and the other two are the upper and lower bands of the moving average line. The upper and lower bands are usually calculated as two standard deviations from the moving average line above and below the moving average line itself.

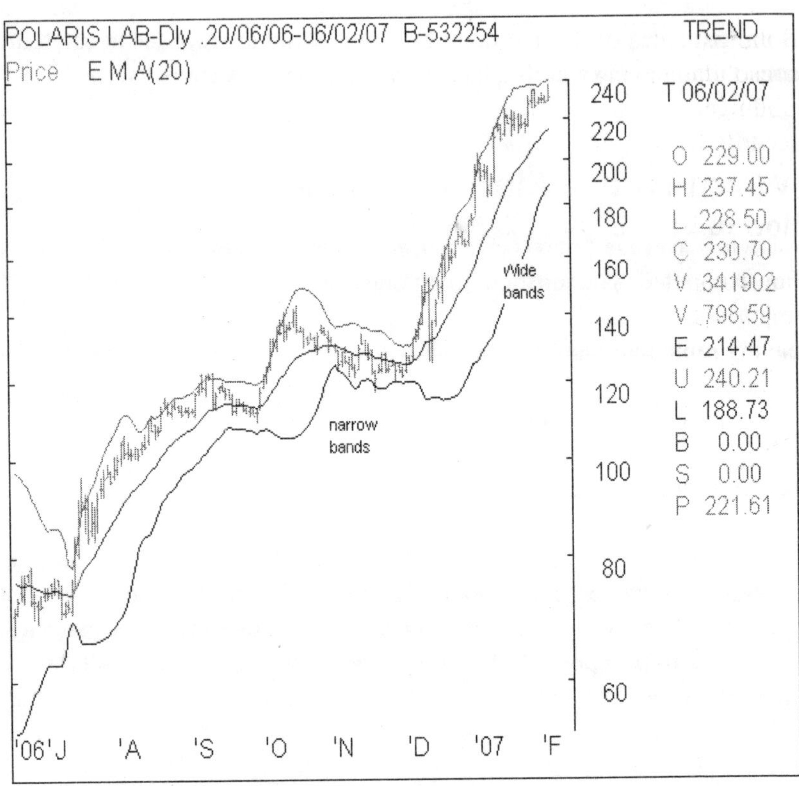

Chart 4.11: **Polaris Software's chart with the Bollinger Bands superimposed on price**

The standard parameter used by John Bollinger was to use a 20-day simple moving average with a standard deviation of two. Chart 4.11 shows a price chart with the Bollinger bands superimposed upon it.

Bollinger bands inform a trader about periods of high and low price volatility. Volatility of a security means the extent of fluctuations in its price over a period of time. If the range of fluctuations is high, then the security is considered as more volatile, and *vice versa.*

Knowing the volatility of a security can help you anticipate whether its subsequent price move will be smaller or larger. Thus, when a security's price is moving in a narrow range (low volatility), the

Bollinger bands will narrow down. This would suggest that prices are consolidating before a bigger move ahead. Conversely, when the Bollinger bands are more widely separated, it indicates that the security has recently been volatile and a cooling-off may be likely.

How to Use Bollinger Bands

For using Bollinger bands effectively, the upper and lower bands are important. Thus when the price touches the upper or lower band after having remained between the bands for some time, it suggests that the market is turning in that direction. If the price rises above the

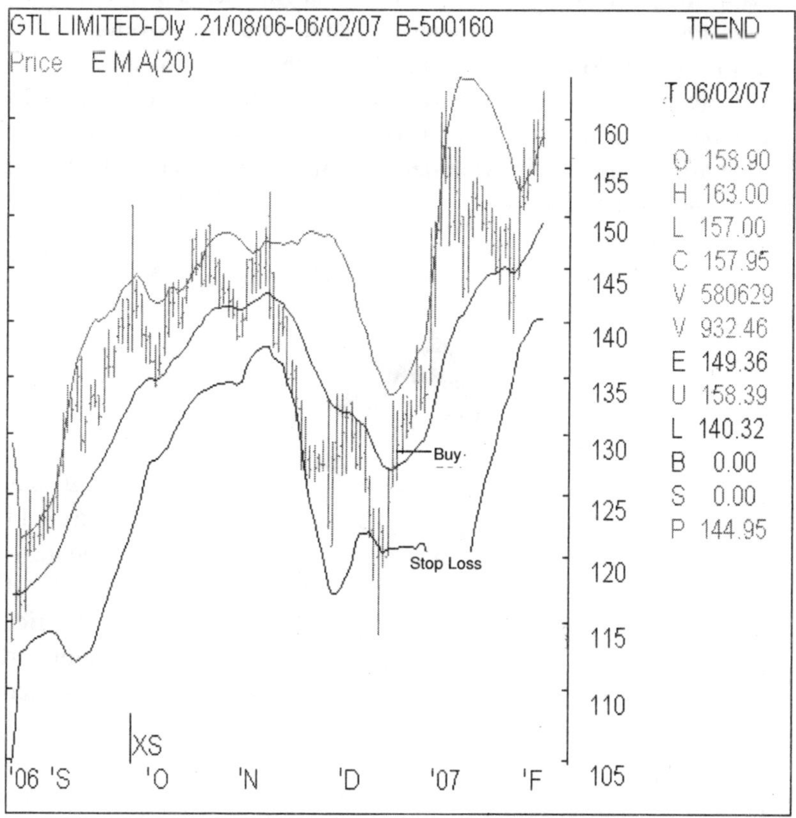

Chart 4.12: **Trading GTL stocks using Bollinger Bands**

upper band, it indicates that it's now headed higher and buying may be initiated. Conversely, if the price falls below the lower band, it's an indication that it is now headed lower and selling, or short-selling, may be initiated.

Many traders use the middle line (the moving average line) as the trigger line for initiating a buy or a sell. The logic is that during up moves or down moves prices have a tendency to find resistance / support at the middle line and so when the middle line 'barrier' is broken it alerts the trader of a likely change in the market sentiment.

Thus, if the price was, say, in a down trend and then closes above the middle line, the aggressive trader may initiate a buy position with a stop loss just below the lower band, and then wait for the price to break out above the upper band. Once the price moves above the upper band, the trader can add to his buy position, expecting the market to become more volatile with an upward bias. Chart 4.12 depicts this phenomenon.

5

The Fibonacci Relevance

'1.618 is often referred to as the "Golden ratio" or the "Divine ratio."'

Ancient Wisdom — The Fibonacci Number Series

In the year 1202, Leonardo Fibonacci discovered an interesting number series while observing rabbits breed. This discovery was further studied and tracked by other observers in later years and has been found to have relevance in many facets of nature.

This number series, called the Fibonacci number series, is derived by adding the previous two numbers to arrive at the next one.

The series thus looks as follows:

0 1 1 2 3 5 8 13 21 34 55 89 144 233, and so on.

Every number in the series is the summation of the previous two numbers. For example, the number 55 is the summation of 21 and 34. Similarly, 144 is the summation of 55 and 89, and so on.

This number series is found to occur in many natural phenomena. The Fibonacci number, and their ratios, are found in many plants, flowers, leaf arrangements, vegetables and fruits. Moreover, it has been observed that even our own galaxy, the Milky Way, follows this number series.

Even the human anatomy is full of Fibonacci numbers or ratios. The core human body has five outlets (two hands, two legs and one head), and each outlet has five other outlets. For instance, the hands and legs culminate in five, in turn, fingers (including the thumb). The head has five 'outlets' in the form of two nostrils, two ears and one mouth.

It should be pointed out that the occurrence of Fibonacci numbers and ratios is not a universal law but instances of its occurrences are large enough that they cannot be ignored.

The Fibonacci number series also has certain interesting relationships and characteristics:

1. The ratio of each number to its previous number tends towards 1.618. For instance, 89 divided by 55 gives 1.618. This Fibonacci ratio, (namely 1.618), is called the divine ratio or the golden ratio.

2. The ratio of each number to its succeeding number tends towards 0.618. Taking the example of 89 again, 89 divided by 144 gives 0.618, and so on.

3. The ratio of each number to its second succeeding number tends towards 0.382. Taking the example of 89 again, 89 divided by 233 is 0.382, and so on.

Use of Fibonacci Numbers and Ratios in Technical Analysis

- Fibonacci numbers are used while defining moving average periods. Thus, instead of taking, say, a 30-day moving average, one may as well use a 34 (Fibonacci) days moving average. Or, instead of a 20-day moving average, one may use the moving average of 21 (Fibonacci) days.

- The second use is in defining market turning points. It is usually found (though not always) that an up or down trend often reverses on Fibonacci days. Thus, if the markets have been falling for a few days, one can expect a reversal on, say, the 5th day or the 8th day.

- The proponents of the Elliot Wave Theory, a more recent branch of technical analysis, extensively use Fibonacci numbers and ratios.

- Fibonacci ratios are used by technical analysts in the retracement theory for determining possible support and resistance areas — more of this in the succeeding pages of this chapter.

Using Fibonacci Numbers for Defining Moving Average Periods

In Chapter 4 we discussed the concept and use of moving averages. Many technical analysts use the Fibonacci number series while defining the periods to use in moving averages:

- Thus for short term periods, traders may use 3-day, 5-day, 8-day or 13-day moving averages.

- For medium term periods, one may use 21-day, 34-day and 55-day moving averages.

- For longer time frames, one may use 89-day, 144-day or 233-day moving averages.

Here it is important to mention that the fact of using a Fibonacci number for constructing a moving average does not necessarily suggest a more effective outcome in terms of profitability. However, a general observation has been that using the Fibonacci number 'may' be more useful.

You would remember that in Chapter 4 we noted that the Sensex shows good medium term direction when it is above or below its 34 DMA. This does not, however, mean that it will be significantly more effective than a 35- or 40-day moving average. Chart 5.01 illustrates a two moving average system using Fibonacci numbers.

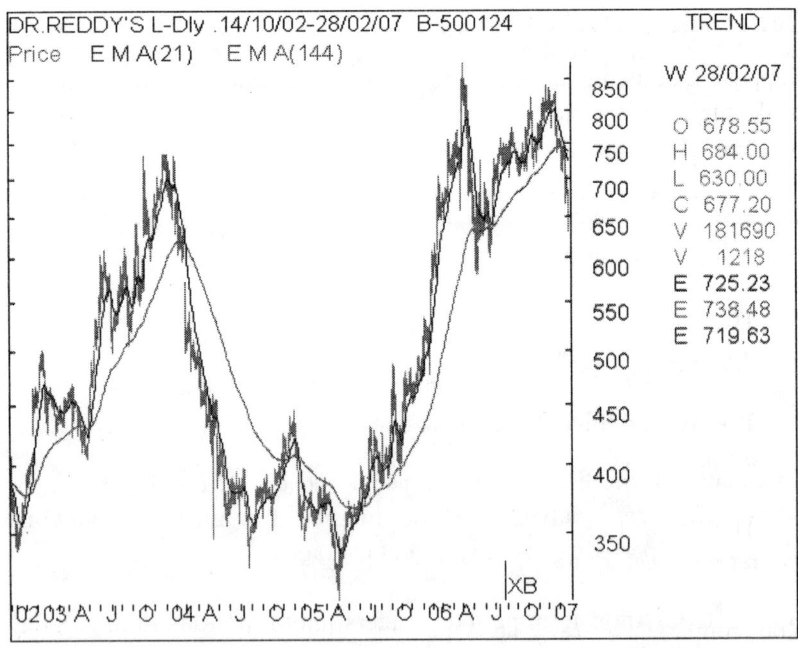

Chart 5.01: **Tracking the long term trend on the chart of Dr Reddy's Laboratories using the two moving average crossover method — the 21 DMA for medium term and the 144 DMA for the longer term. Both 21 and 144 are Fibonacci numbers.**

Using Fibonacci Ratios in Retracement Theory

The Retracement Theory

As discussed in this chapter the retracement theory seeks to identify the likely levels from where prices may retrace their path.

The basics of trend analysis hold that any price move — whether up or down — will have intermittent corrections. As you would recall from Chapter 2, corrections are small price movements which are counter to the main trend.

Many a time the trader faces a dilemma as to the extent of the correction. It is here that the retracement theory comes handy.

Retracement Levels in an Up Trend

Suppose that the price trend is up. Now, after making an intermediate peak (high), prices start falling (correction) because of profit booking by some players who may have bought at lower levels.

The retracement theory suggests the following three price levels till where the price might retrace (in this case, fall) during the correction:

- The first level is a 38.20% correction, or retracement, of the original price move.
- The second level is a 50% correction, or retracement, of the original price move.
- The third (and important) level is a 61.80% correction, or retracement, of the original price move.

You might have observed that the first and third retracement percentages are Fibonacci ratios.

Example 5.1

Computation of Retracement Level in an Up Trend

Suppose a stock has risen from a level of, ₹ 135 to a peak (high) of ₹ 312, thus moving up by ₹ 177. The retracement price levels till where the price may fall in the ensuing correction are calculated as under:

Retracement level 1:

Peak price – (Price move × 38.20%)

₹ 312 – (177 × 0.382)

₹ 312 – 67.60 = ₹ 244.40, **say ₹ 245.**

Retracement level 2:

Peak price – (Price move × 50%)

₹ 312 – (177 × 0.50)

₹ 312 – 88.50 = ₹ 223.50, **say ₹ 225.**

Retracement level 3:

Peak price – (Price move × 61.80%)

₹ 312 – (177 × 0.618)

₹ 312 – 109.4 = ₹ 202.60, **say ₹ 205.**

Chart 5.02: **Tata Steel's chart indicating the retracement levels over a long time period and the long price move involved. These levels will broadly tell the trader where support is likely when the price starts moving down.**

Chart 5.02 of Tata Steel depicts one such example of retracement using real market data of Tata Steel.

Retracement Levels in a Down Trend

Suppose that the price trend is down. Now, after making an intermediate low, prices start rising (correcting) because of squaring-off of short sold positions by some traders who may have sold at higher levels.

The retracement theory suggests the following three price levels till where the prices can retrace (in this case, rise) during any ensuing correction:

- The first level is a 38.20% correction, or retracement, of the original price down move.
- The second level is a 50% correction, or retracement, of the original price down move.
- The third (and important) level is a 61.80% correction, or retracement, of the original price move.

Example 5.2

Computation of Retracement Level in a Down Trend

Suppose a stock has fallen from a level of, ₹ 128 to a low of ₹ 69, thus moving down by ₹ 59. Now in a corrective up move, the retracement price levels till where the price may rise are calculated as under:

Retracement level 1:

Low price + (Price move × 38.20%)

₹ 69 + (59 × 0.382)

₹ 69 + 22.50 = ₹ 91.50, **say ₹ 90.**

Retracement level 2:

Low price + (Price move × 50%)

₹ 69 + (59 × 0.50)

₹ 69 + 29.5 = ₹ 98.50, **say ₹ 98.**

Retracement level 3:

Low price + (Price move × 61.80%)

₹ 69 + (59 × 0.618)

₹ 69 + 36.40 = ₹ 105.40, **say ₹ 105.**

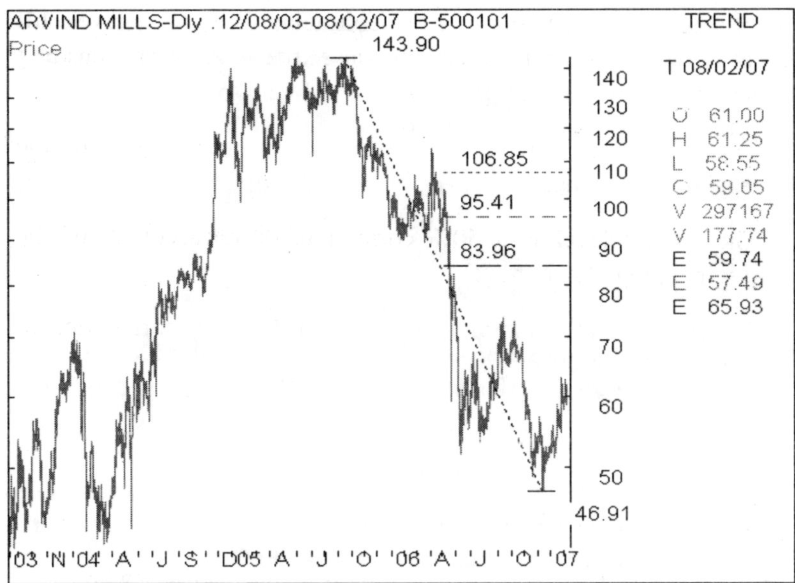

Chart 5.03: **Arvind Mills' chart showing retracement levels in the case of a down trend. You will observe that after touching a high of ₹ 144, the scrip was in a down trend and touched a low of ₹ 47. The scrip has since stabilized and is trying to go back up. The trader can determine the broad price levels where the up move may face resistance in this by calculating the retracement levels.**

Chart 5.03 depicts one such example of retracement in a down trend using real market data

Some Practical Observations on Retracement

It has been observed that the extent of correction or retracement can be used to predict whether the resumption of the price movement in the direction of the ongoing trend, subsequent to the correction, will be fast or slow. Here is how:

- When the price retraces or corrects about 38.20% (first level) of the immediate previous price move, and then resumes its move in the direction of the original trend, it is likely to be a fast move towards a new high or new low, as the case may be.

- In case the price retraces or corrects about 50% (second level) of the immediate previous price move, and then resumes its move in the direction of the original trend, it is likely to be a normal speed move towards a new high or low, as the case may be.
- But if price retraces or corrects about 61.80% (third level) of the immediate previous price move, and then resumes its move in the direction of the original trend, it is likely to be a slow move towards a new high or low.
- Finally, a price close beyond the 61.80% level (third level) would usually suggest an exhaustion of the original ongoing trend, or at least a weakening of the basic trend.

Chart 5.04 indicates how the Sensex moved after a 50% correction. Typically when a security retraces only up to 50%, then the subsequent up move will be large and relatively fast.

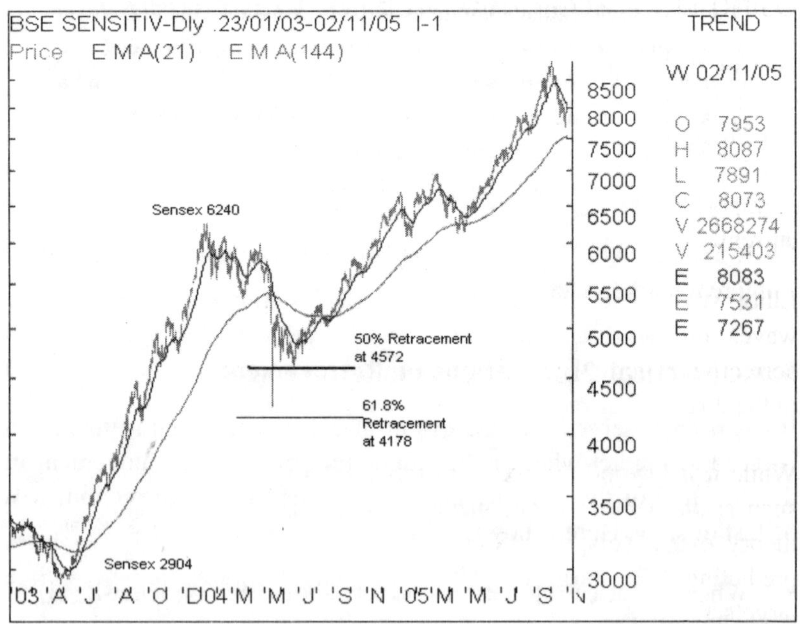

Chart 5.04: **Chart showing a 50% retracement of the Sensex during the May 2004 sell-off and its subsequent rally beyond 8,500**

Gann's Retracement Levels

William Gann, the creator of the Gann Theory, believed in breaking down a price move in 'eights' in order to determine the retracement levels. Thus the retracement levels in this case will be computed as $1/8^{th}$, $2/8^{th}$, $3/8^{th}$ and so on equivalent to 12.50%, 25%, 37.50%, 50%, 62.50%, 75% , 87.50% and 100%.

You can observe that the 37.50% ($3/8^{th}$) and the 62.50% ($5/8^{th}$) retracement levels are very near to the Fibonacci retracement levels of 38.20% and 61.80%.

Also in the retracement theory examined earlier in this section, we have in fact taken the Gann retracement level of 50% as one of our important retracement levels.

Using Fibonacci Ratios in Elliot Wave Theory

One of the newer areas of study in the technical analysis of price charts is the Elliot Wave Theory. This theory suggests that market movements can be visualized as having wave-like patterns and just like it is important for a trader to know in which trend the market is, it is important for an Elliot Wave analyst to know as to which wave is currently in progress.

Elliot Wave Theory suggests that markets move in basically five waves in the direction of the trend, followed by a three-wave corrective pattern. Thereafter one witnesses another five-wave pattern in the direction of the trend, and so on.

While it is beyond the scope of this book to go into a complex topic such as the Elliot Wave Theory, it is pertinent to mention that the theory extensively uses Fibonacci numbers and ratios, not only in predicting price targets but also in analyzing and predicting time targets.

For instance, once a five-wave pattern in the up direction is completed, the subsequent correction (in the opposite direction) would usually take support at 61.8% before prices again start another five-wave pattern. Chart 5.05 depicts one such formation on the gold futures chart.

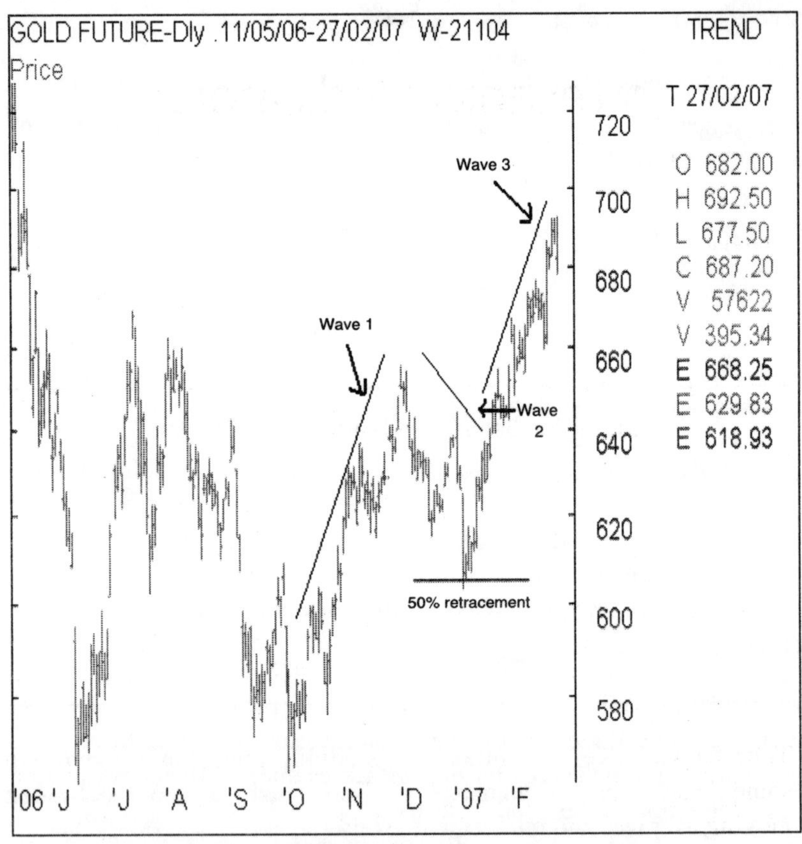

Chart 5.05: **Gold futures chart depicting Elliot Wave Theory. Typically, Wave 2 retraces 61.80% of Wave 1. In the above case, the price retraced only 50% and started moving back up to make Wave 3.**

6

Technical Indicators

The Tools of the Trade

'There are two things infinite — the universe and human stupidity. I am not sure of the former.'

– Albert Einstein

Thus far we have concentrated on studying price charts along with some basic tools of technical analysis, such as trend definition, moving averages and retracement levels.

The advancement of technology and the extensive use of computers have equipped traders and investors with more sophisticated tools for understanding and profiting from the behavior of prices.

Statistical indicators are among such sophisticated tools that we can use. The values of these indicators are derived from the main price data, using simple statistical methods.

Usually, and also usefully, indicators are depicted either below or above the main price chart. This helps in tracking the movement of both prices and an indicator simultaneously and thus understand their relationship better.

Distinction Between Indicators and Oscillators

Here it would be useful to note the distinction between an indicator and an oscillator. Though many use these terms interchangeably, it may be noted that on account of their method of computation, oscillators are those indicators whose values tend to oscillate between a fixed range, usually from 0 to 100.

Thus, all indicators are not oscillators but all oscillators are essentially indicators. Indicators, therefore, is a much broader term which encompasses oscillators.

How to Use Technical Indicators

Technical analysts use indicators for the following main reasons:

1. Indicators help in identifying overbought and oversold market conditions.

2. Indicators help in judging the strength of a price move.

3. Indicators may often provide early signals of a trend reversal.

Let's try to understand each of these aspects in a little more detail.

1. Identifying Overbought and Oversold Market Conditions

The first and foremost use of an indicator is that it reveals whether a price move, whether up or down, is nearing exhaustion. Oscillators are typically more useful for this purpose but even non-oscillating indicators can also detect such conditions.

An overbought condition is said to exist when the price run-up has been continuous and / or rapid, after which prices often take some rest. **On oscillators, an overbought condition is depicted when the value of the oscillator rises above 75 (in a range of 0 to 100).**

An oversold condition exists when the price fall has been continuous and / or fast, suggesting that prices now may take some rest. **On oscillators, an oversold condition is depicted when the value of the oscillator falls below 25 (in a range of 0 to 100).**

Traders may want to define other values for their own trading purposes. This decision of using other values also depends on the type of oscillator / indicator selected.

Chart 6.01 depicts both an overbought and an oversold condition with the help of an oscillator.

Readers may note that the overbought and oversold value criteria of 75 and 25, respectively, are not sacrosanct and can be appropriately altered by a user of price charts to suit his / her own requirements. Thus, for your trading purpose you may consider 70 and 30 as the value criteria for overbought and oversold conditions.

Caution

Oscillators work better in a non-trending market. In a strongly trending market, oscillators may remain in overbought or oversold zones for long periods and this may not foretell any pause in the price trend

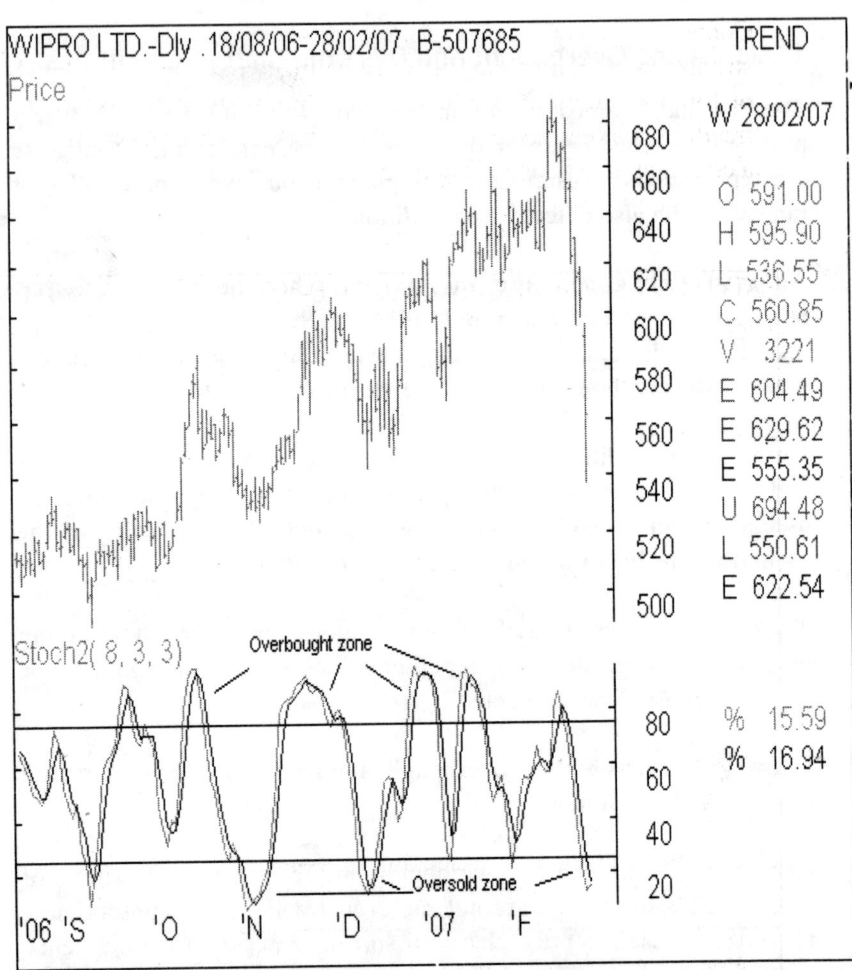

Chart 6.01: **Chart of Wipro Ltd. showing overbought and oversold conditions on an oscillator**

Thus, an oscillator may remain in the overbought region (say above 75) for a long time in a strongly bullish market.

Conversely, it can remain in the oversold region (say below 25) in a strongly bearish market. This must be treated as one of the drawbacks of following only an oscillator, which normally works better in non-trending markets, also called trading markets. Chart 6.02 depicts such a condition in a strongly trending market.

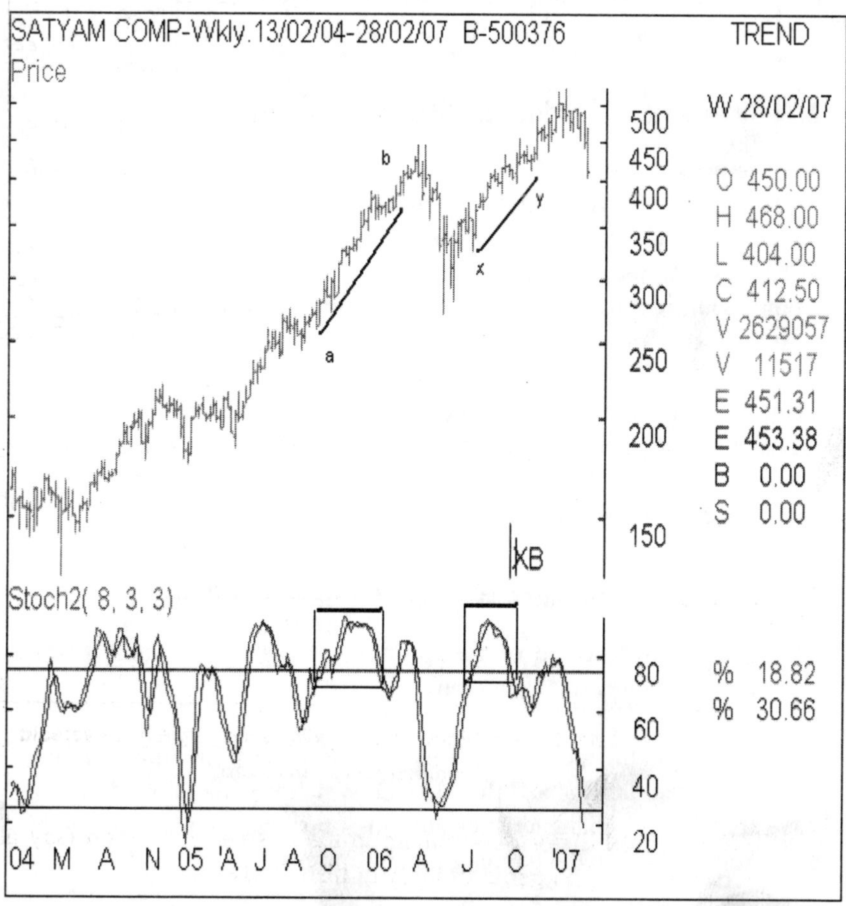

Chart 6.02: **Satyam Computers trending strongly. You will observe that even though the oscillator was in overbought condition the prices rallied during the period marked from 'a' to 'b'. A similar instance is observed during the period marked from 'x' and 'y'.**

In strongly trending markets it is not uncommon to see such price rises or price falls even when the oscillators are in overbought or oversold conditions.

Strong trending markets are better traded using other trend following indicators, such as MACD, rather than with oscillators like the stochastic. We shall learn more about these indicators and the methods of using them in the following sections.

2. Indicators Help Judge the Strength of a Move

The second use of an indicator is to suggest to an analyst the strength of the ongoing move. Suppose a trader has bought a stock or security when it started to rise from a low level accompanied by appropriate technical parameters giving a buy signal. The dilemma now is as to when should the trader book profit. Should he sell for a 5% gain, or wait for a 10% move, or a 25% move?

The use of indicators helps in addressing such a dilemma. Many trend following indicators can keep you in a trade for a longer time, ensuring that you do not exit too early. In subsequent sections we shall consider one such common indicator.

3. Indicators as Advance Warning Signals of a Reversal

The third important use of indicators is to warn an analyst of an impending price reversal situation.

This is where the concept of divergence comes into play. Many indicators, like the RSI and the MACD (which we shall now discuss), have 'predicting' characteristics and often provide advance signals of any likely change in the ongoing trend of prices.

Concept of Divergence

As mentioned above, one way of using an indicator is to watch out for early warning signals they provide of an impending price reversal. The concept of divergence is central in this regard.

A divergence is said to occur when the price movement and the indicator movement are not in tandem, i.e. they are not synchronized. When such a divergence takes place, it should warn you that something is amiss since the price and its indicator are not moving together. Either the price, or the indicator, is wrong.

There are two types of divergences — positive divergence and negative divergence.

Positive Divergence

A positive divergence occurs when during a down trend the price makes a new low but the indicator does not do so. It may have made either an equal or a higher low at the time when the price was making a new low (*see* Chart 6.03).

The occurrence of a positive divergence suggests to longer term investors or traders that the market's intermediate bottom may have been touched and it could be time to buy into the security for an expected re-bound.

The Psychology Behind Positive Divergence

The psychology behind the possibility of a change in trend as depicted by a positive divergence is that the most recent new low made by the price may possibly have been a result of panic selling by market players.

In other words, the market may have overplayed the bearish or weak sentiment and that the market's reaction was extreme. This possibility is revealed to an analyst by the indicator's refusal to fall further and make a new low.

Practical Hint for Trading a Positive Divergence

On Chart 6.03, there is a portion marked 'swing'. In order to actually trade the positive divergence, i.e. to buy the security based on the assumption of an impending reversal, you should wait for the indicator to break above this swing level. Once the swing is broken, it gives a confirmation of the positive divergence.

You can observe on the price chart that while the price made a new low, the RSI indicator (which we shall study in Chapter 7) made a higher low during the same period.

This suggests a conflict, i.e. divergence between the price move and the indicator movement, giving an early signal to the trader that either

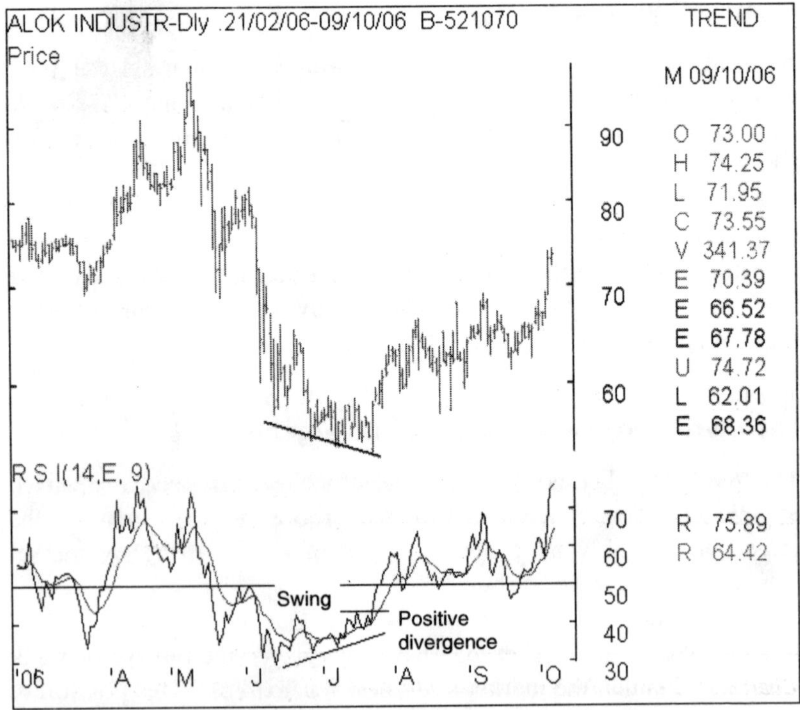

Chart 6.03: **Chart of Alok Industries Ltd. showing a positive divergence**

the price or the indicator is wrong. Thus, the trader should become skeptical of the ongoing trend (in this case, the down trend) and wait for signs of a reversal.

Negative Divergence

A negative divergence occurs when during an up trend, the price, makes a new high but the indicator fails to similarly make a new high. It may have made either an equal, or a lower high at the time the price was making a new high. Chart 6.04 depicts an example of negative divergence.

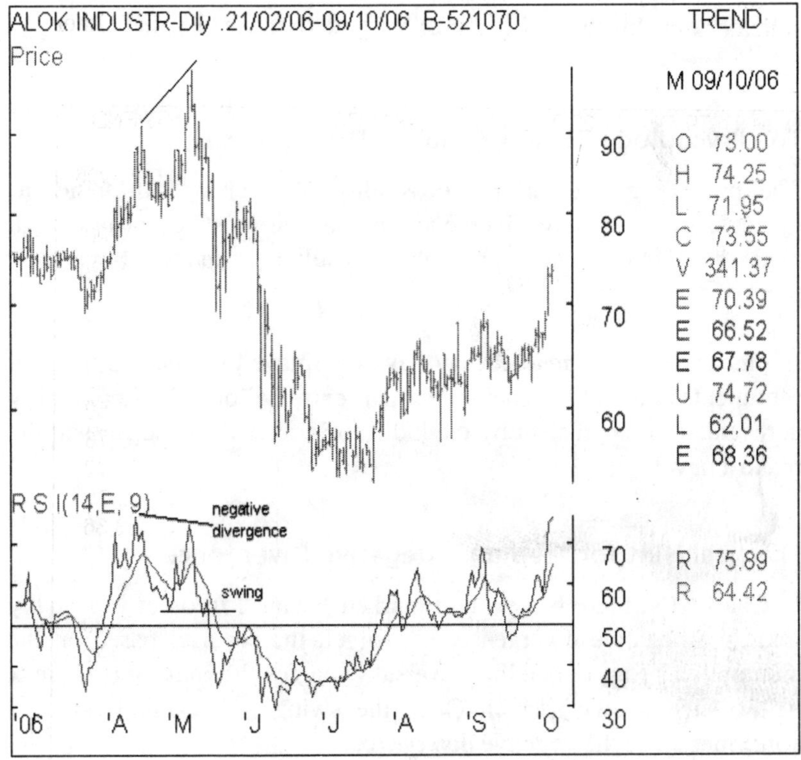

Chart 6.04: **Chart of Alok Industries Ltd. showing negative divergence on the RSI indicator**

The occurrence of a negative divergence suggests to longer-term investors or traders that the market's intermediate top may have been touched and it may be time to sell the security as the price is expected to fall.

You can observe on the Chart 6.04 that while the price made a new high, the RSI indicator on the other hand, made a lower high during the same period.

This suggests a conflict between the price move and the indicator movement, an early signal to the trader that either the price or the indicator is wrong. At such a time, a trader would become skeptical of the ongoing up trend and wait for signs of a reversal. The subsequent price down move confirmed the signal given by the negative divergence.

The Psychology Behind Negative Divergence

The psychology behind the possibility of a change in trend, as depicted by a negative divergence, is that the most recent new high made by the price was probably a result of euphoric buying by players.

In other words, the market may have overplayed the bullish or good sentiments and that its reaction was an 'extreme' one. This possibility is revealed to the analyst by the indicator's refusal to rise further and make a new high.

Practical Hint for Trading a Negative Divergence

In Chart 6.04, there is a portion marked 'swing'. In order to actually trade the negative divergence, i.e. to sell the security based on the assumption of an impending reversal, wait for the indicator to break below such a swing level. Once the swing is broken, it gives a confirmation of the negative divergence.

Typical Characteristic of RSI Divergence

When an RSI divergence occurs in an overbought area, namely when a negative divergence occurs, and is confirmed by a swing breakout as explained above, the price move will be such as to take the RSI value to the oversold zone. When an RSI divergence occurs in an oversold area, namely when a positive divergence occurs, and the divergence is confirmed with a 'swing' breakout as explained above, the price move will be such as to take the RSI value to the overbought zone, respectively.

This characteristic of the RSI divergence is useful for traders and investors to know when they should watch for signals of booking profit.

Chart 6.05 provides an example of a positive divergence in the chart of Arvind Mills.

Chart 6.05: **Positive divergence in the chart of Arvind Mills**

You will observe in Chart 6.05 that after the positive RSI divergence, the 'swing' breakout gave a buy signal; the price move was such that the RSI went into the overbought region.

Technical Indicators and Their Signal Lines

For entering or exiting a trade, one can use any of the indicators singly, including the three which will be studied in detail in Chapter 7. This is made possible by the use of signal lines on the indicators.

A signal line is a moving average of the indicator itself. Thus, along with plotting the indicator in the lower panel of a price chart, we can 'superimpose' on the indicator graph, its own moving average line.

For example, when a standard 14-day RSI (Relative Strength Index) indicator is plotted in the lower panel of the price chart, a 9-day moving average of this 14-day RSI can be superimposed on it to generate buy and sell signals:

- When the RSI line crosses its 9-day moving average line from below, a buy signal is generated suggesting to the trader to initiate a buy position.
- Conversely, when the RSI line crosses its 9-day moving average line from above, a sell signal is generated suggesting to the trader to initiate a sell position.

Chart 6.06 depicts the indicator and its signal line.

Buy and sell signals generated by indicators will prove to be more profitable when traded under certain conditions. The method using the indicators and their signal lines for trading is suggested in subsequent sections.

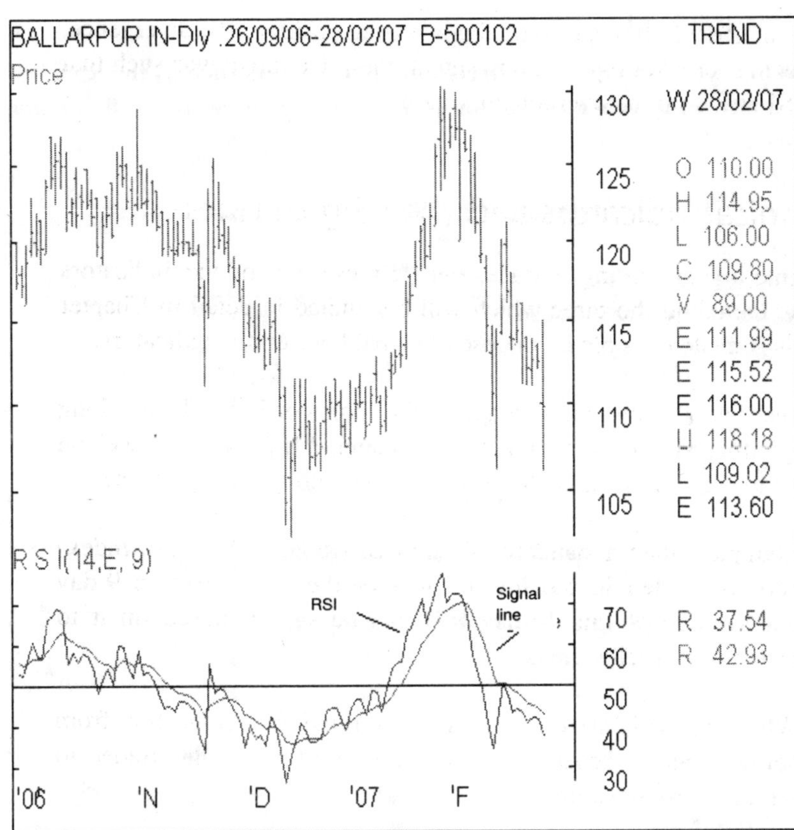

Chart 6.06: **Chart of Ballarpur Industries Ltd. showing the RSI indicator along with its signal line. The signal line is nothing but the 'n' period moving average of the RSI itself.**

Trend Line on Indicators

Just as we draw trend lines on price charts, we can similarly draw trend lines on indicators.

Thus, just as we draw a rising trend line on a price charts by joining the higher lows, we can similarly draw a rising (support) trend line on a price indicator by joining the higher lows of the indicator. The converse is true for resistance lines, or falling trend lines.

Practical Hint

When we see a trend line breakout on indicators such as the RSI, it is usually an advance indication of the corresponding trend line being broken by the price.

Chart 6.07 of Gold Futures (in US$) illustrates a case in point.

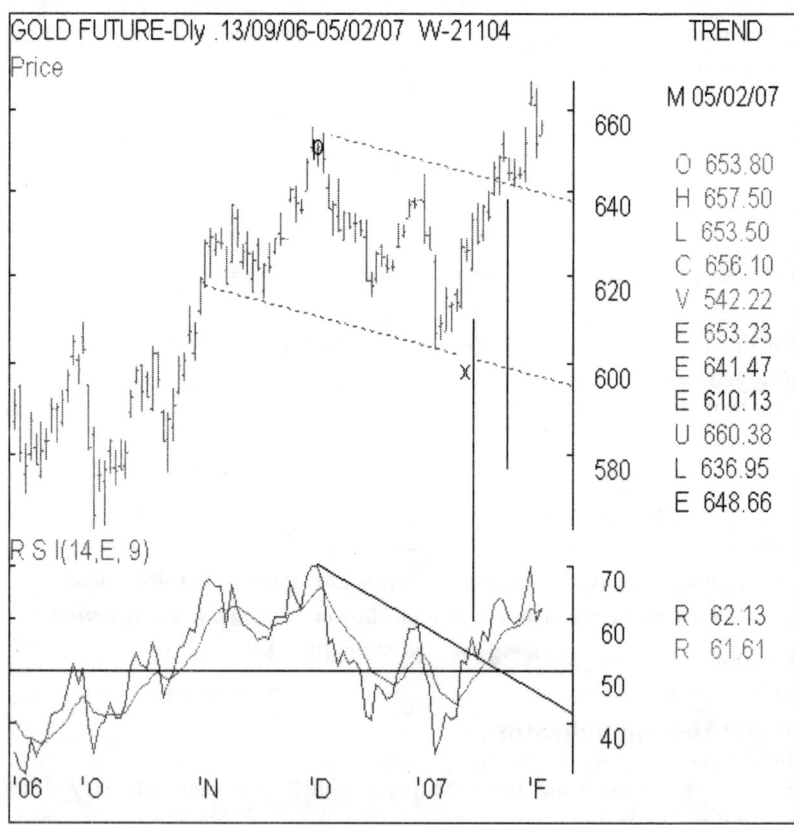

Chart 6.07 : **Chart of gold futures (in US $) showing an advance breakout on the RSI indicator — the price breakout occurs after a time lag of about 5 days. Usually it has been observed that the time lag between the indicator breakout and the price breakout is about two days.**

In Brief: Market Indicators

Apart from stock-specific indicators which will be discussed in Chapter 7, there are certain indicators which provide some insight about the market's mood as a whole. These are commonly known as market breadth indicators. **It is better to confirm the indications provided by such market breadth indicators with the help of other specific indicators before acting on them.** These indicators essentially show you the market's direction and strength rather than providing any actual trading signals.

The 52-Week High-Low Indicator

This indicator tracks, on a continuous basis, the number of stocks which have made their yearly highs and yearly lows, and thus provides an idea of the strength of the market's current direction.

For instance, when markets are rising, a larger number of stocks make new yearly highs suggesting strength. However, if the 52-week high-low indicator is not rising in a rising market, you should become cautious and seek confirmation from other specific indicators.

Advancing / Declining Issues

This indicator tracks, on a continuous basis, the number of stocks that have advanced and the number that have declined. The interpretation is similar as in the case of the high-low indicator in the sense that in a rising market there should logically be more stocks which are advancing (rising) than are declining. If this is not the case, a trader should become cautious about a market's move.

Advancing / Declining Volume

This is a variant of the advancing / declining issues indicator. In this case the volume (number of shares traded) of the advancing and declining stocks are tracked to ascertain whether the market's movement is accompanied by corresponding volume or not. The interpretation will be that in a rising market there should logically be more stocks which are advancing (rising) with a higher volume, than are declining. If this is not the case, the trader should become cautious about the market's move.

Many other market breadth indicators have been developed using similar concepts (with some variations), such the On-Balance Volume (OBV), the Cumulative Volume Index (CVI), the McClellan Oscillator, etc. The interpretation of these indicators remains more or less the same and each needs to be confirmed by other specific indicators.

7

The Basic Indicators

'There is no bull side or bear side of a market. There is only the "right" side.'

– Jesse Livermore, legendary trader.

The Stochastic Indicator (Oscillator)

The RSI (Relative Strength Index) Indicator

The MACD (Moving Average Convergence Divergence) Indicator

Chapter 6 introduced the basics of interpreting statistical indictors. In this chapter we shall consider three common and widely used indicators, at first singly and then try to understand the relationship among the three in order to arrive at a meaningful sense of price movements.

The first indicator we shall discuss is the Stochastic which is an oscillator in the real sense of the term. As explained in the previous chapter, this type of an indicator is more useful and profitable during fluctuating or trading markets but not during a strongly trending one.

The second indicator can be termed as a 'semi-trending' indicator — the RSI. Though it is essentially an oscillator, it lends itself to be used even as a trending indicator. How this can be done is discussed and explained.

The third indicator is a trend following indicator — the MACD, which has the capacity to catch major trends but may not be able to give profitable results in non-trending markets.

These indicators have been chosen with the purpose of analyzing the various phases of the market, both to gain the maximum in a trending market, and also preventing losses in a non-trending phase of the market.

The detailed computation of these indicators is beyond the scope of this book. But you don't worry about that since all charting software will generate these indicators for you. What is important is to understand their application in comprehending the market's behavior.

The Stochastic Indicator (Oscillator)

Invented by George Lane, the stochastic indicator is an oscillator which tries to measure the relative position of the closing price usually at the end of a day, or for any other predefined period. To be more precise, it tracks whether the day's or the selected period's closing price was nearer to the day's (period's) low or nearer the day's (period's) high.

The logic of this indicator is that during a price up move, the price should close nearer the day's highs, while during a down move, it would close nearer the day's lows.

When the closing price is nearer the day's low instead of nearer the day's high during an up trend, or when in a down trend the closing price is nearer the high (rather than the day's low), it is a warning to the trader that the ongoing move is growing weak.

The indicator tries to track this 'mood' in the form of a graph.

The indicator plots two lines, namely — % K and % D.

The % K line is the faster line while the % D is the slower one and is used as the signal line. Thus when % K line crosses the % D line from below, the stochastic oscillator generates a buy signal and, conversely, when the % K line crosses % D line from above a sell signal is generated.

Computation of the Stochastic Indicator

The basic computation of the % K and % D values is as follows:

% K = 100 * [(C – Ln) ÷ (Hn – Ln)]

where

C = Closing price

Ln = Lowest low of the last n days

Hn = Highest high of the last n days.

% D = 100 [H3 ÷ L3]

where

H3 = 3-period sum of {C – Ln}

L3 = 3-period sum of {Hn – Ln}

We can observe that the % D line is actually a 3-period smoothened average of % K line.

Most traders use a variant of this stochastic oscillator called the **slow stochastic**. The slow stochastic is arrived at by eliminating the % K line and treating the % D line as the % K line, and then further smoothening this 'new' % K line to find the new % D.

Readers need not worry about the mathematics of this calculation as most software today provides the facility of plotting the slow stochastic.

Chart 7.01 provides an example of a price chart along with the slow stochastic.

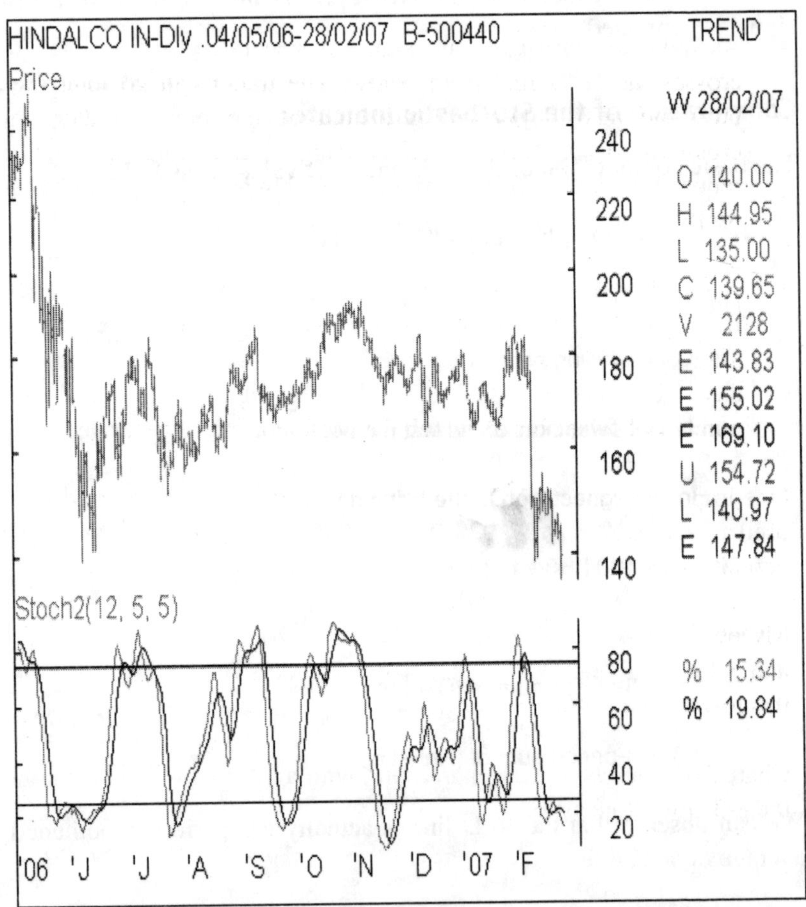

Chart 7.01: **Price chart of Hindalco along with its standard stochastic indicator (oscillator). The darker line on the stochastic indicator is the signal line while the lighter line is the indicator itself.**

How to Trade Using the Slow Stochastic Oscillator

One simple and popular way of using the slow stochastic oscillator is to trade on the crossover of the % K and % D lines:

- As indicated above, a buy signal is generated when % K line crosses the % D line from below. The trader can go long (i.e., buy) the next day above the high of the previous day (the crossover day). This sort of filtering is advisable in order to reduce the number of false signals which may be generated by the oscillator.

- A sell signal is generated when % K line crosses the % D line from above. The trader can then go short (i.e., sell) the next day after below the low of the previous day, namely the crossover day. This sort of filtering is advisable in order to reduce the number of false signals which the oscillator might generate.

One important issue which can be mentioned here is the period to be used for calculating the % K and % D lines. Most software have a default value of 12 and 5, respectively, for % K and % D lines.

My own preference is to use a lower time frame. I use the values 8 and 3 for % K and % D, respectively. Readers may want to validate this lower time frame.

Chart 7.02 depicts a price chart along with a 12-5 slow stochastic and the 8-3 slow stochastic.

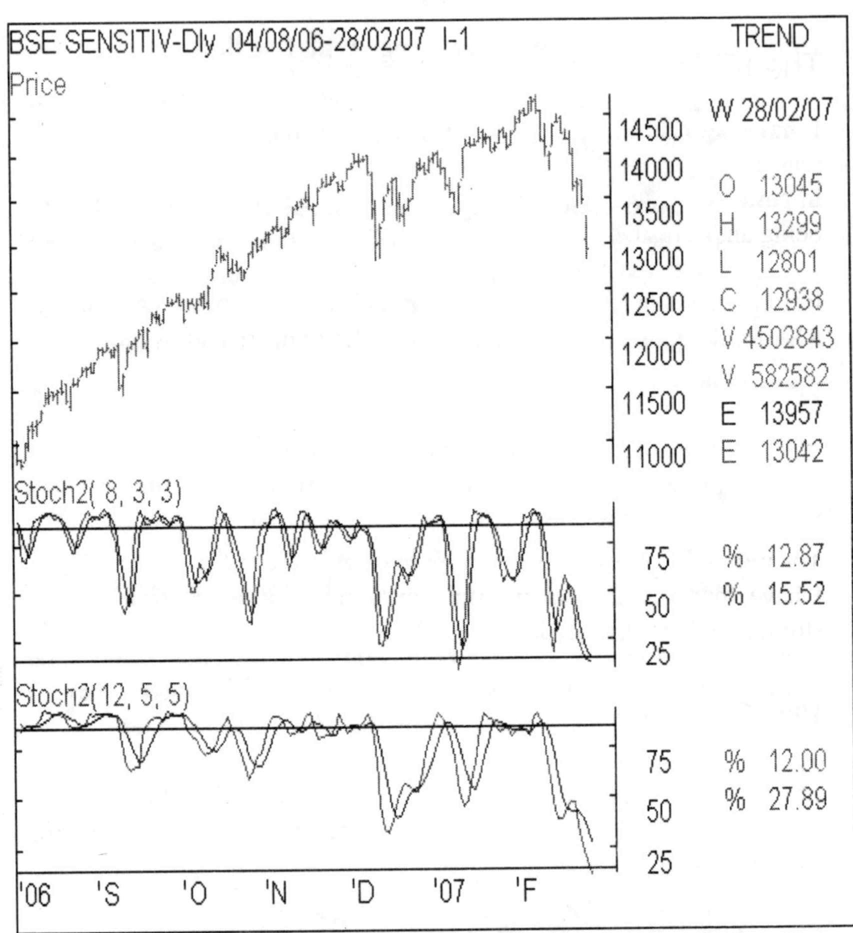

Chart 7.02: **A chart of Sensex showing two stochastic indicators of different periods. One is the standard period stochastic used in most software as default and the other is a lower period stochastic which I use. Obviously, the lower period stochastic will be more volatile than the standard one. My own experience with the lower period stochastic when used along the basic trend is more than satisfactory.**

The RSI (Relative Strength Index) Indicator

I have specifically chosen RSI as the second oscillator for two reasons. One is that it is quite popular but second, and more important, because of its potential of being a trend identifier despite being an oscillator.

Before we delve further into the intricacies as to how we can use the RSI oscillator as a trend identifier, let us first understand its basics.

Developed by Welles Wilder, RSI compares the magnitude of a stock's recent gains to the magnitude of its recent losses. Thus, it tracks whether the extent of the recent gain in price is higher than the extent of its recent losses.

The number of days for the RSI suggested by Welles Wilder is 14 and I have found it quite appropriate on various types of securities — stocks, bullion, agro products, metals, etc.

The RSI Formula

The basic formula for the RSI is as follows:

$$\text{RSI} = 100 - 100 / (1+\text{RS})$$

$$\text{First RS} = \text{Average Gain} / \text{Average Loss}$$

$$\text{Smoothened RS} = \frac{\{\text{Previous Average Gain} \times 13 + \text{Current Gain}\} / 14}{\{\text{Previous Average Loss} \times 13 + \text{Current Loss}\} / 14}$$

Where;

$$n = \text{Number of RSI periods}$$

$$\text{Average Gain} = \text{Total of gains} / n$$

$$\text{Average Loss} = \text{Total of loss} / n$$

It may be appropriate to mention here that the phrase 'relative strength' can be misleading. The indicator does not compare different shares or sectors — as the word relative may suggest. Like any other oscillator, RSI is a derivation of the price data.

Chart 7.03 shows the price chart of Ballarpur Industries along with its standard 14-day RSI.

RSI and Its Signal Line

Like any other indicator, the RSI can, if required, be used as a trading tool. Thus buying and selling signals can be generated from this indicator by using a signal line.

To achieve this, usually a 9-day moving average line of the RSI is superimposed on the RSI line. The crossover of these lines generates the required signals.

Thus:

- When the RSI line cuts its 9-day average line from below, a buy signal is generated and the trader can enter long (buy) the stock.
- Conversely, when the RSI line cuts its 9-day average line from above, a sell signal is generated and the trader can go short (sell) the stock.

Chart 7.03 also shows the price chart and RSI along with its signal line.

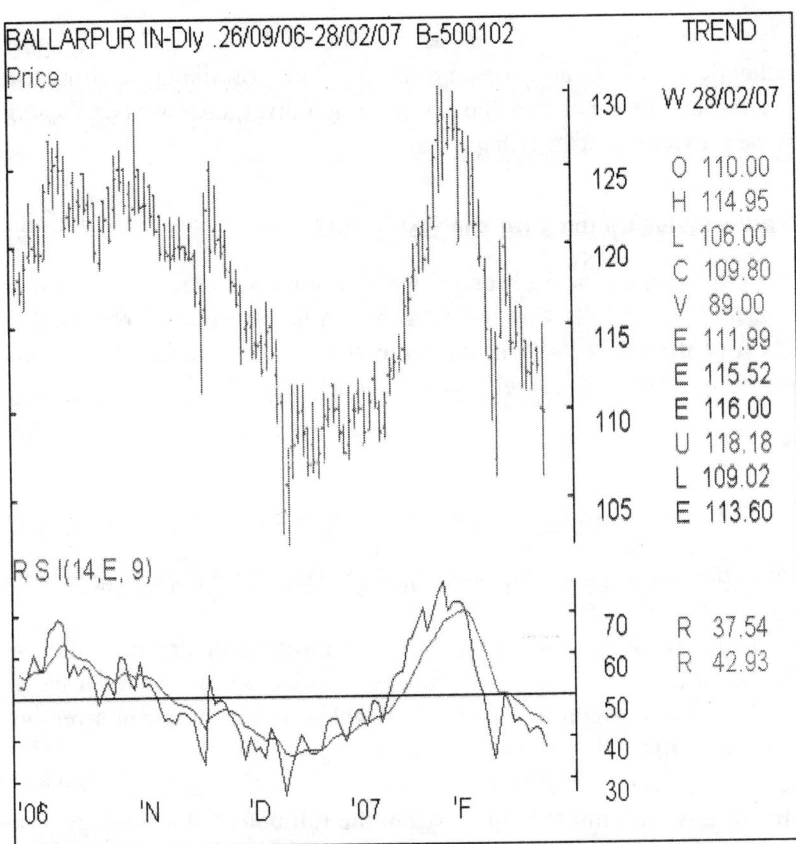

Chart 7.03: **Price chart of Ballarpur Industries with its standard 14-day RSI indicator**

How to Trade Using RSI

The standard methods of using RSI would be to trade on its signal line, or to look out for a divergence on the indicator. My own observation, however, has been that it is not too profitable to trade the signal line since this can throw up far too many trading signals which results in losses and increased transaction costs (mainly brokerage).

However, **divergences on the RSI do prove to be useful, especially in suggesting 'exhaustion' of the ongoing trend.** A divergence of the price move and its RSI can be considered by the trader as more authentic than a divergence on a more volatile oscillator, such as the stochastic. The general method of trading a divergence was explained in the previous chapter (Chapter 6).

Trading Divergences on the RSI

Over the years I have observed with various securities that when a security rises or falls with a divergence in the overbought region, the subsequent price move will have the strength to take the RSI to the overbought / oversold level, as the case may be.

Thus:

- If a stock confirms a negative divergence after a good price run up, the subsequent price down move will usually have the strength to take the RSI value to the oversold region below 30.
- Conversely, if a stock confirms a positive divergence after a significant price fall, the subsequent price up move will usually have the strength to take the RSI value to the overbought region above 70.

This observation might help you gain the full potential advantage of a trade and not take profit too early during the fall. Here it will be important to remember that divergences are advance warning signals of possible trend reversals. And, if the trend does reverse, the price move will be larger than usual and hence potentially more profitable.

Chart 7.04 depicts such a phenomenon. Readers may want to validate this by observing different charts in various markets.

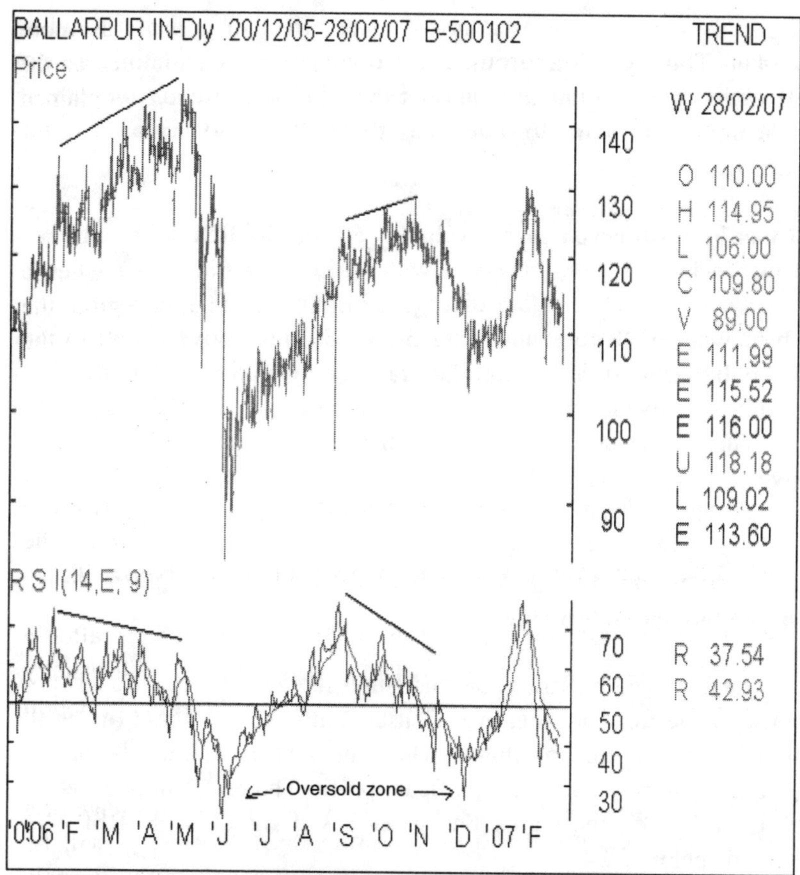

Chart 7.04: **Chart of Ballarpur Industries showing how a negative divergence on the RSI in the overbought zone 'leads' to a price fall which takes the RSI value to the oversold zone. Incidentally, there are two such instances on the price chart — something which is rare.**

RSI — An Oscillator which Can Identify Trends

As mentioned earlier, one important reason for choosing RSI as one of the three indicators was that despite being an oscillator, it also has the potential to identify trends.

Remember, usually an oscillator is more effective in a non-trending market. Thus, when a strong trend is underway, oscillators are not effective and technical analysts would use trend identifying indicators. The RSI, however, has the potential to act as a trend-identifier as well.

It has been observed that a value of 50 for the RSI is effectively a trend decider.

Thus, when RSI goes and stays above 50, i.e. above its mid point value between 0 and 100, the trader may consider the trend as positive. Consequently, a sell signal (using the signal line) on this oscillator when the RSI is above 50 may be ignored, as it may not give significant profit. The better strategy would be to buy when the signal line gives a buy signal while RSI value remains above 50.

Thus, the broad strategy is — when RSI is above 50, ignore the sell signals but act on buy signals.

Conversely, when RSI goes and stays below 50, the trader may consider the trend as negative. Consequently, a buy signal (using the signal line) on this oscillator when the RSI is below 50 may be ignored as it may not give significant profit. The better strategy would be to sell when the signal line gives a sell signal while RSI value remains below 50.

Thus your broad strategy is — when RSI is below 50, ignore buy signals but act on sell signals. Chart 7.05 of Ranbaxy Laboratories depicts a price chart and its RSI.

Chart 7.05: **Price chart of Ranbaxy Labs with its RSI. You will note in the above chart that whenever the RSI value goes above 50, the corresponding price up move is marked with a thicker up arrow while whenever the RSI falls below 50, it is marked with a thinner down arrow. This should give you a visual picture of the trend identification capability of the RSI indicator. A trader would be more comfortable trading long in a bullish market condition (thick up arrow) and more comfortable selling in a bearish market condition (thin down arrow).**

The MACD (Moving Average Convergence Divergence) Indicator

The MACD is a trend-defining indicator. It is not an oscillator as its computation can, theoretically, take any value.

MACD is calculated as the difference of two moving averages. This difference is then plotted as the MACD indicator.

One of the moving averages used in the calculation is of a shorter term and the other one of a longer term. During the course of the price action these two moving averages will, at frequent intervals, have a tendency to converge or diverge. This also means that the difference of these moving averages (defined as MACD) will have a tendency at times to approach zero and at other times to move away from zero. Accordingly, the MACD moves around the zero line.

The MACD thus gives a visual picture of the convergence and divergence of the two selected moving averages.

Chart 7.06 shows the price chart of Larsen and Toubro along with its MACD.

The usual parameters (as defined by its developer Gerald Appel) are to consider the 12-day moving average as the shorter term average and 26-day moving average as the longer term one.

The standard MACD is the difference of the 12 DMA and the 26 DMA with a superimposition of the 9 DMA of the MACD to be used as the signal line. These figures are marked on the indicator panel as (12, 26, E, 9). Here 'E' stands for exponential moving average in Chart 7.06.

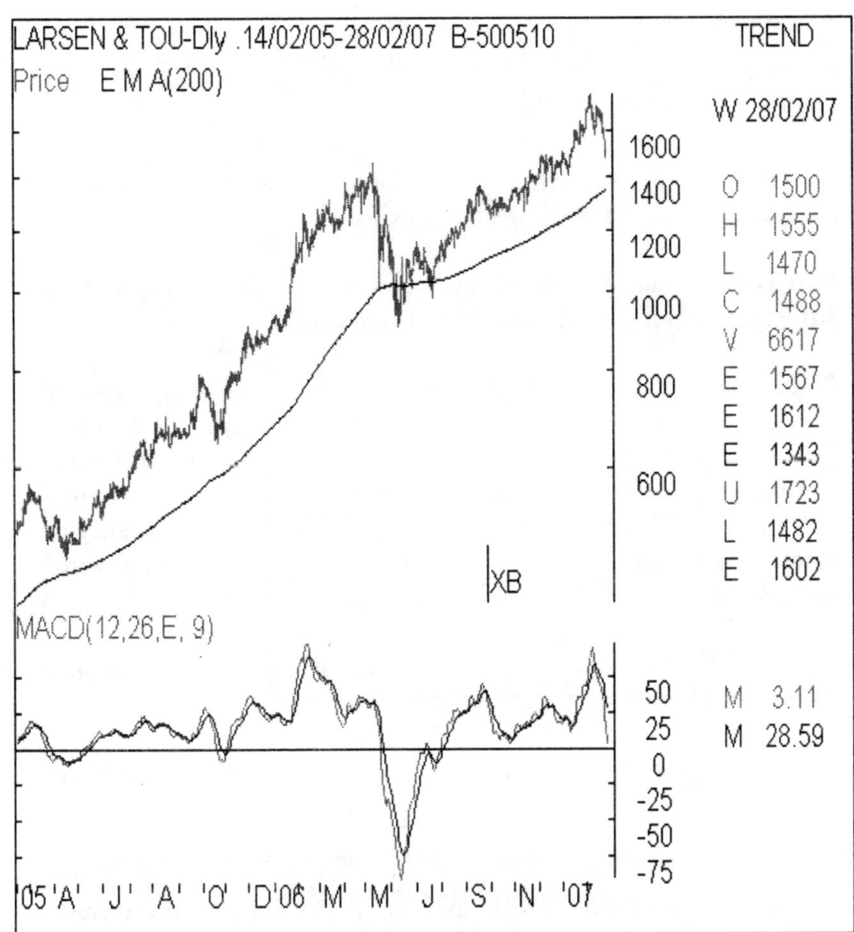

Chart 7.06: **Price chart of Larsen and Toubro along with its standard MACD**

You may, however, want to test other periods depending on your trading time frame. Thus, a short term trader may, for example, use, say, 5 days as the short term period and 10 days as the longer term period. Obviously such shorter than usual term moving averages will converge and diverge more frequently.

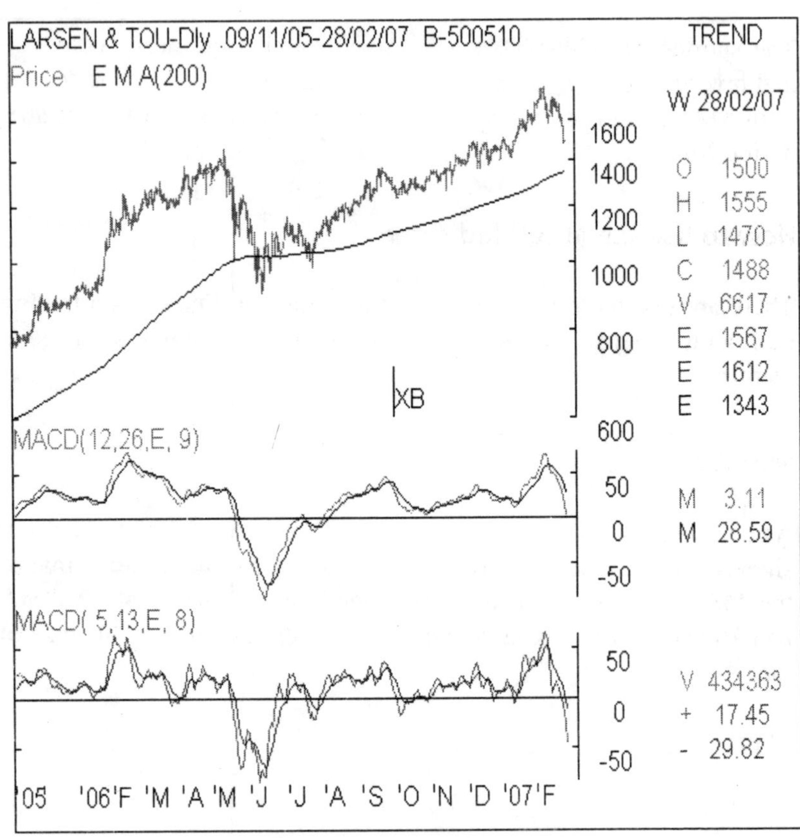

Chart 7.07: **Price chart of Larsen and Toubro with both its standard MACD and a shorter term MACD**

Chart 7.07 shows the price chart of Larsen and Toubro with both a standard MACD and a shorter term MACD.

It is important to mention here that the difference is always calculated as 'shorter term moving average minus the longer term moving average'

Thus, when we use the standard periods, the MACD will be computed as 12 DMA minus 26 DMA.

The shorter term MACD will be more volatile and hence converge and diverge more often. Another way of saying this is that the shorter term MACD will cross the zero line more often than will the longer period MACD.

How to Use the MACD Indicator

There are two basic ways of using this indicator. One is as a trading tool with the use of the signal line, and the second as a trend identifier.

MACD as a Trading Tool

As a trading tool, one may use the MACD for generating buy and sell signals. This can be done by superimposing a moving average line of the MACD itself. When using the standard parameters of 12 DMA and 26 DMA, it is normal to superimpose a 9-day moving average of the MACD.

Thus:

- A buy signal is generated, when the MACD line crosses the signal line — namely, the 9-day moving average of MACD — from below. Traders using this method may want to use the filter of buying on the day after the crossover if the price rises above the signal day's high.

- A sell signal is generated, when the MACD line crosses the signal line from above. Traders using this method for trading may want to use the filter of selling the day after the crossover if the price falls below the signal day's low.

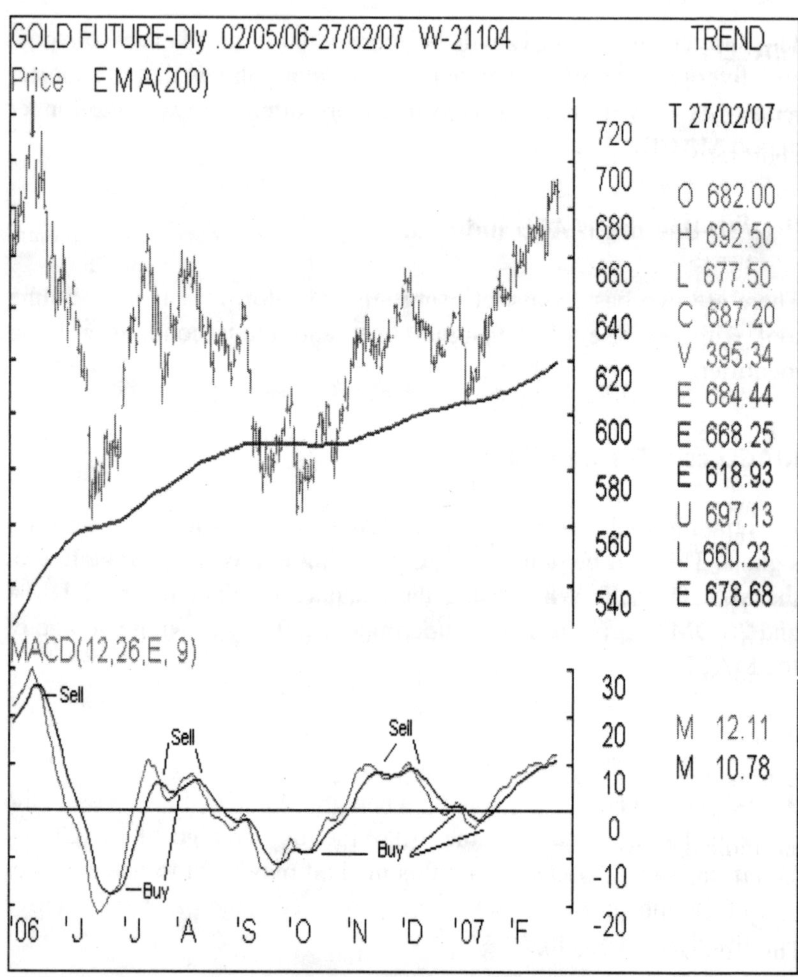

Chart 7.08: **Chart of gold futures (in US $) showing the MACD with buy and sell points based on signal line.**

Chart 7.08 shows the use of MACD as a trading tool using the signal line.

MACD as a Trend Identifier

The MACD indicator works quite admirably as a trend identifier for short term trading. Let us see how:

- When the MACD is above the zero line, it implies that the short term moving average is higher than the longer term moving average — remember, the MACD is calculated as the shorter term moving average minus the longer term moving average.

  Another way of understanding this is that in the shorter term prices are moving higher than they were in the longer term. And so in the shorter term the market has turned more bullish than it was in the longer term. This mood of the market is captured by the MACD's position being above the zero line.

- The converse is true when MACD is below zero line. It implies that the short term moving average is lower than the longer term moving average and hence in the shorter term the market has turned more bearish than it was in the longer term.

During the price action, if the MACD starts falling from above the zero line and crosses below it, and the price movement gathers, it is an indication of a change in trend from bullish to bearish. The converse is also true.

Thus, the zero-line crossover on the standard MACD could be treated as trend identifier. When the MACD is above the zero-line, the security may be considered bullish and when it is below the zero-line, it may be treated as bearish.

Chart 7.09 illustrates the use of MACD as a trend identifier.

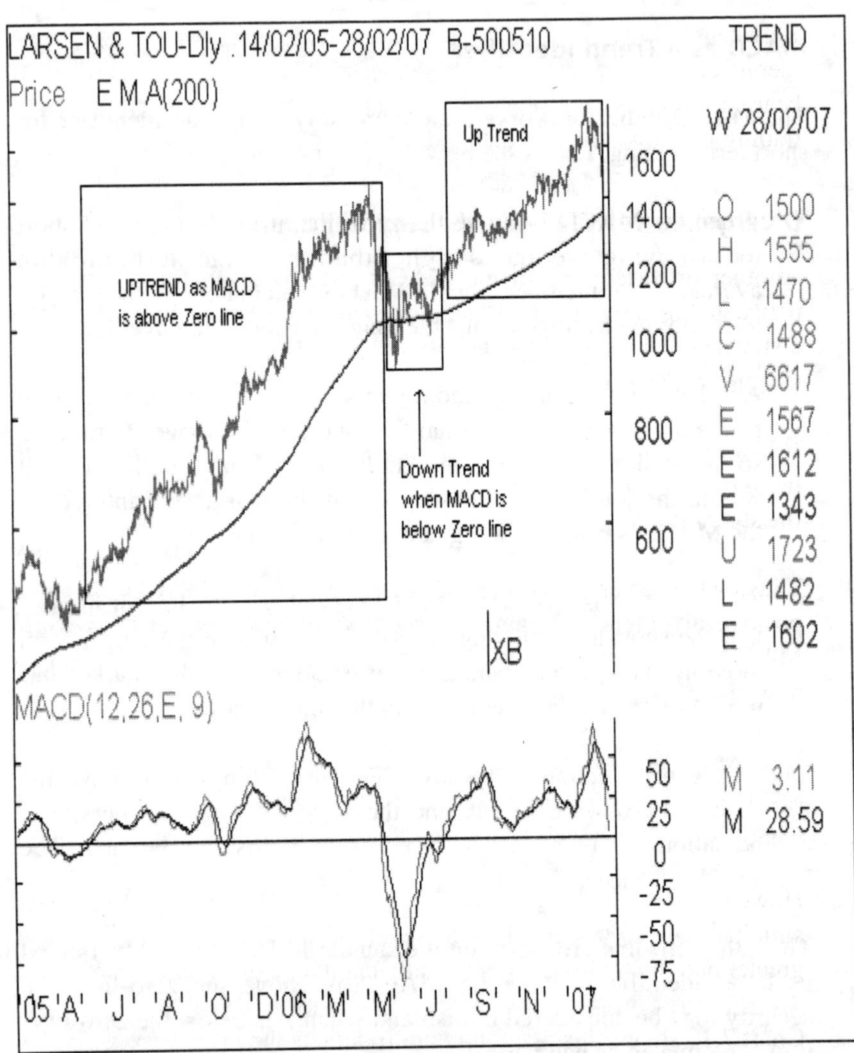

Chart 7.09: **Up trend and down trend on the chart of Larsen and Toubro as suggested by the MACD indicator. When the MACD is above the zero line it indicates an up trend and when it is below the zero line, it is a down trend.**

Between the two methods of using MACD, I prefer using it as a trend identifier. Once I know whether a particular security is bullish or bearish, I can use the other oscillators to tell me when to trade. This trading method is further detailed in the following sections.

Divergence Between the MACD and Price

Another important use of the MACD is to look out for divergences between the movement of the price and its MACD indicator. The concept of positive and negative divergences was explained in Chapter 6.

It has been observed that divergences appearing on the MACD are far more reliable than those appearing on other oscillators, such as the stochastic or RSI.

Thus, when after a consistent fall in prices the MACD shows a positive divergence — namely, when prices make newer lows while MACD does not, it is a strong warning signal that the trend might now change.

It is pertinent to note here that during a particular point in time, a security may be showing a divergence on, say, the RSI but it may not necessarily show a divergence on the MACD.

However, when both RSI and MACD show divergence simultaneously, the confidence level of an impending reversal is greater and the trader can confidently capitalize on such opportunities.

Chart 7.10 shows this phenomenon. It depicts the price chart of HPCL along with the RSI and MACD indicators which are both in divergence.

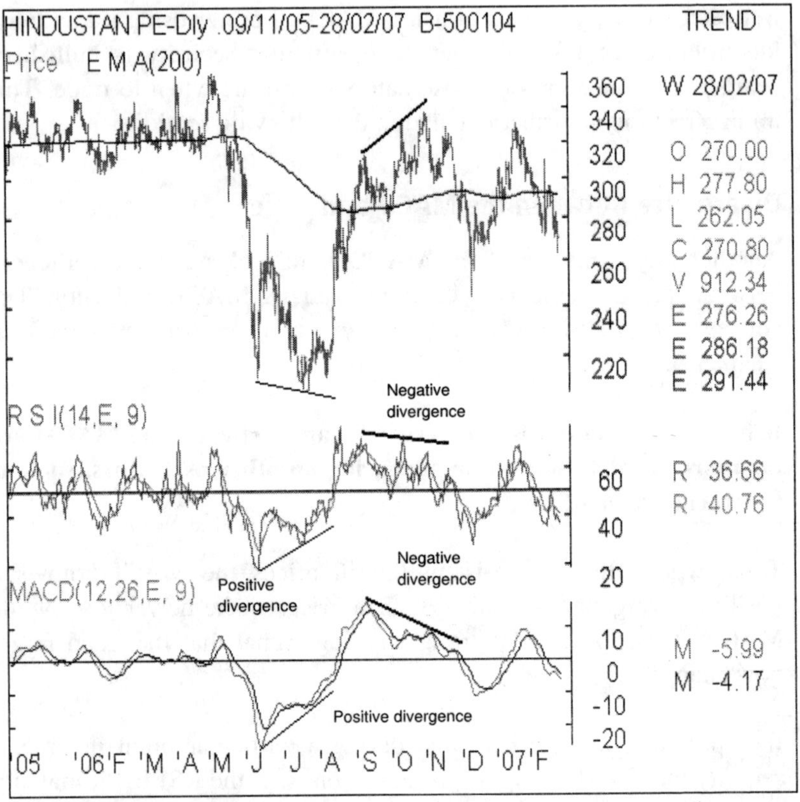

Chart 7.10: **HPCL chart showing a positive divergence on both RSI and the MACD. It also shows a negative divergence on both RSI and MACD. When both the RSI and MACD are showing similar divergence with the price, the confidence of a trend reversal increases**

8

Combining the Technical Tools

'I can calculate the motions of the stars, but not the madness of crowd.'

– Sir Isaac Newton

Tata Steel (formerly Tisco) Ltd.

Arvind Mills Ltd.

The previous chapters introduced the basics of technical analysis. My attempt was two-fold. One was to introduce you to this scientific study of prices in as lucid manner as possible and, secondly, to be careful that only such material is introduced as is necessary at the basic level.

For instance in Chapter 7, I touched upon only three out of the numerous indicators available to a trader today, courtesy the computer revolution. I believe that the mere availability of a wide choice of indicators is no reason for studying them all. One negative of today's computer age is that there is an overload of information, but that is not the same thing as knowledge. I believe this observation applies equally to a study of the markets.

In their quest to find the holy grail, an ultimate solution, traders the world over keep inventing newer indicators, only to find that they are no nearer to that ultimate solution than they were before they invented it. The situation is akin a computer loop which it goes round and round searching for a solution, which remains ever evasive.

Which is why I chose the three indicators that I did. There are among the most widely used ones and are also easy to understand and interpret. In this chapter we are going to combine the knowledge of the preceding chapters and mould it into a meaningful analysis which you can use for any price chart. I have used such analyses on various markets, such as the Indian stock market, international stock markets, commodities, forex, *et al*, and believe that the step by step approach explained below is useful in comprehending any price chart.

Methodology

We shall take a particular security's price chart and then approach it step by step as follows:

Step 1: Defining the basic trend of the security.

Step 2: Drawing trend lines with important support and resistance price levels for future reference.

Step 3: Incorporating short term, medium term and longer term moving averages on the price chart to help us get a better perspective of the price behavior.

Step 4: Determining price levels using the retracement theory.

Step 5: Adding indicators — to actually 'tell' us what to do with the security, i.e. whether to buy or sell.

For better understanding, we shall study one example of a security which could be turning down after a bullish phase; and another which was bearish and could be turning up. This will assist you in analyzing both bull and bear markets, up trends as well as down trends.

Example 1

Tata Steel (formerly Tisco) Limited

(A scrip which was bullish — or in an up trend)

Step 1: Defining the Security's Basic Trend

Before even thinking of trading any security, it is very important for a trader or the investor to know how its price has behaved in the recent past; in other words, to figure out the recent trend in its price. As we have studied in earlier chapters, when a security's price makes a higher highs and higher lows formation it is said to be in an up trend — and when it makes a lower highs and lower lows formation, it is said to be in a down trend.

As you would observe from Chart 8.01, Tisco made its low in September 2001 and thereafter was in an up trend right till the date of this analysis (February 2007).

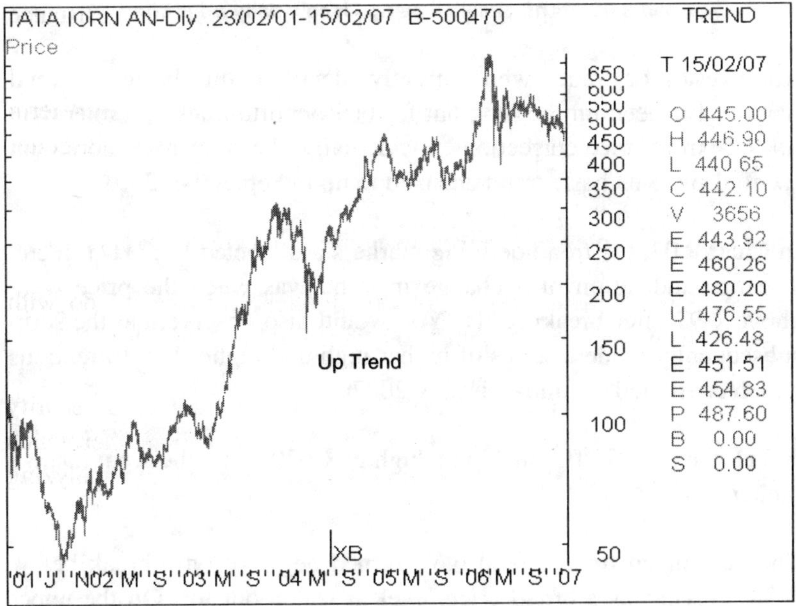

Chart 8.01: **Daily price chart of Tisco indicating up trend**

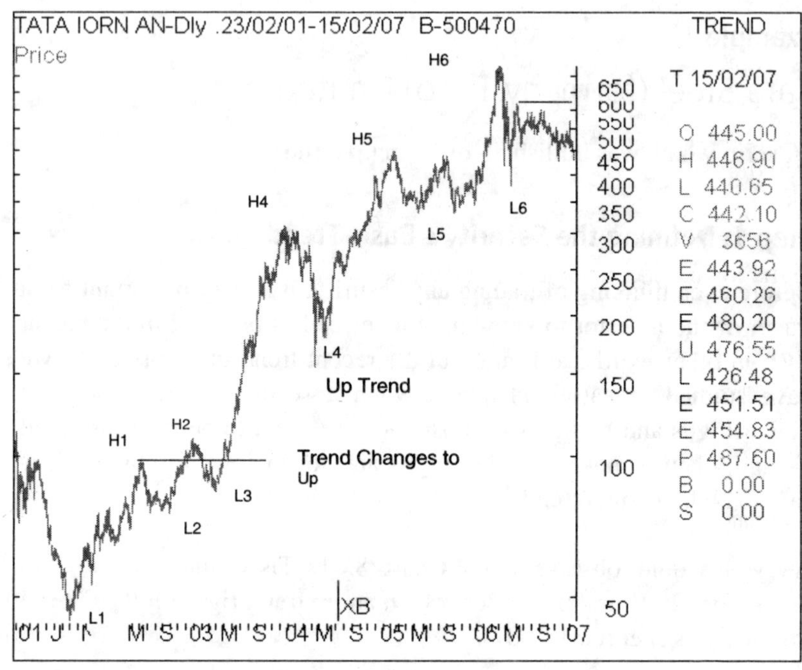

Chart 8.02: **Trend analysis using Tisco's daily price chart**

An investor or trader who correctly identified this basic up trend would have been on the look out for buy opportunities — rather than sell or exit at price corrections. Incidentally, the scrip rose more than six-fold since its basic trend changed to up in September 2001.

In Chart 8.02, the trend defining markers are labeled L1, H1, L2. etc. The first indication of a change in trend was when the price went above ₹ 97 after breaking H1. You would also observe that the scrip subsequently made a series of higher high and higher low formations which continued till mid-February 2007.

In February 2007 after making a high of ₹ 679 (H6), the scrip made a higher low at ₹ 387 (L6).

The current up trend would have turned negative on a break below ₹ 387, giving us a broad price level to watch out for. On the upper side, the most recent high (after the ₹ 387 low) is marked by a horizontal line at the price value of ₹ 567. This level should therefore be viewed as important because if it is not broken on the upside, it may give us the first indication of a lower high formation — a prerequisite for a change in the up trend.

Thus, we now have two broad price levels to watch out for — ₹ 387 on the lower side, and ₹ 567 on the upper side.

Step 2: Drawing Trend Lines With Major Support and Resistance Areas

Once you know that the trend is currently up, you can draw the basic trend lines, namely support and resistance lines, for early warning. Let us consider Chart 8.03.

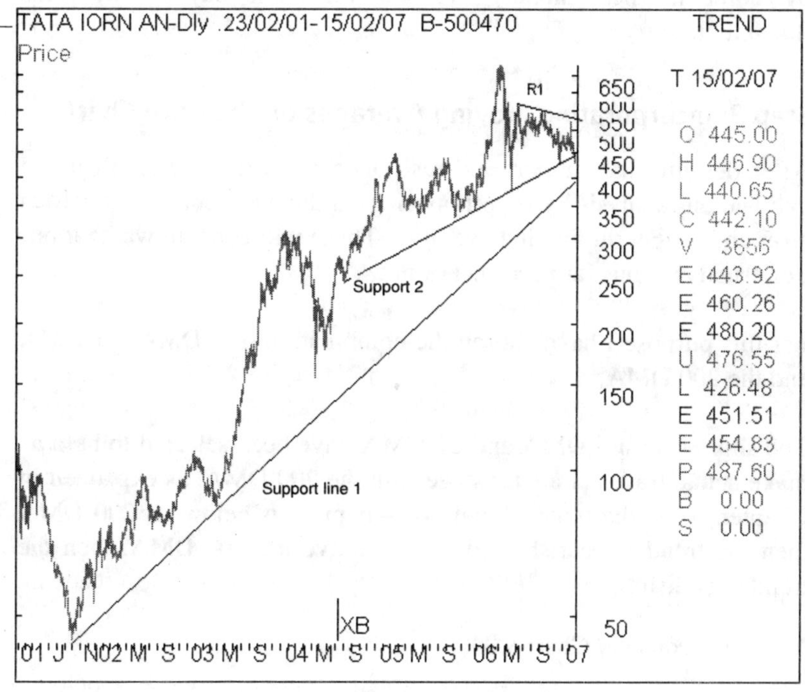

Chart 8.03: **Tisco's daily price chart indicating support and resistance lines**

Support Line 1 indicates the basic support line which captures the entire up trend. This support line has a crucial support level at ₹ 400. This you will note is quite near to L6 (₹ 387) on Chart 8.02.

The medium term support line is shown as Support 2. This gives an indication of the immediate support level at ₹ 440. As you would note, this level was lately broken in intra-day.

The resistance line R1 shows the medium term resistance to the price at ₹ 521.

Thus, for a medium term trader, the upper and lower levels are ₹ 521 and ₹ 440.

Defining such support and resistance levels enables a trader to overcome needless anxiety over the inevitable day to day price fluctuations.

Step 3: Incorporating Moving Averages on the Price Chart

After defining the support and resistance trend lines, we will try to validate our analysis by superimposing on the price chart the medium term and long term moving averages. These will confirm whether our trend analysis thus far is correct or not.

For this purpose I have chosen the combination of 5 DMA, 21 DMA and the 200 DMA.

The shorter-term 5 DMA and 21 DMA have been selected to help us make actual trades at a later stage. But the 200 DMA, as explained in Chapter 10, is the trend identifier — if price is below its 200 DMA then the trend is bearish, and if it is above the 200 DMA, then the trend is bullish.

Now let's consider Chart 8.04.

Chart 8.04: **Tisco daily price chart with moving averages**

You will observe that the 200 DMA has been a reliable trend-decider and would have kept a trader in the market throughout its bullish phase. At the recent juncture, the price is hovering below the 200 DMA and, in fact, the 200 DMA is offering a resistance to any price up move.

Also, the medium term moving average 21 DMA, has crossed the 200 DMA from above, suggesting caution since prices are not sustaining at higher levels and are, in fact, showing some weakness.

One can also visualize that a price fall below ₹ 400 would confirm this moving average sell signal to be a strong one. This price level of ₹ 400 was also incidentally our support line 1 indicated on Chart 8.03.

Step 4: Determining Price Levels Using the Retracement Theory

Readers will recall the retracement theory we discussed in Chapter 5. The retracement levels this theory provides are a rough guide as to the levels where prices are likely to find support in their downward journey, or resistance in their upward journey.

Let's, consider Chart 8.05.

You would note that the retracement levels have been indicated separately for a clearer view. The first price support area is ₹ 438 which has already been broken on the chart.

Chart 8.05: **Tisco daily price chart with retracement levels**

Also, in the panic sell off after making a high of ₹ 679, the price fell nearly to the 50% retracement level of ₹ 363 (the actual low it made was ₹ 387).

My observation has been that if the price spends a lot of time around the 50% retracement, it is suggestive of further ensuing weakness. The logic is that retracement levels are support areas, i.e. temporary resting places for prices before they again start their upward journey. But if the price starts spending more time in a temporary resting place, it would suggest that it may not continue its upward journey but could, in fact, be planning to reverse.

Step 5: Adding Indicators to the Price Chart

Now for a final picture of the current price situation and what to do next, we will add indicators, namely the slower RSI and the trend decider MACD to the price chart.

Chart 8.06 shows the price chart along with these indicators. You may note that in this case we have chosen the weekly chart since the time period of our analysis is long. Also, for the time being I have taken only RSI and MACD in the indicator panel for explanation purpose.

You will note that during the major part of the up trend (as defined by the trend analysis and 200 DMA), the RSI more or less remained above the mid-point level of 50. Lately, however, it has spent more time below the 50 RSI levels, which could be a cause of worry for medium and long term investors.

Earlier, a rise above 50 RSI level coupled with RSI rising above its signal line offered good price up moves to the trader. However, things appear to be turning weak at the current juncture.

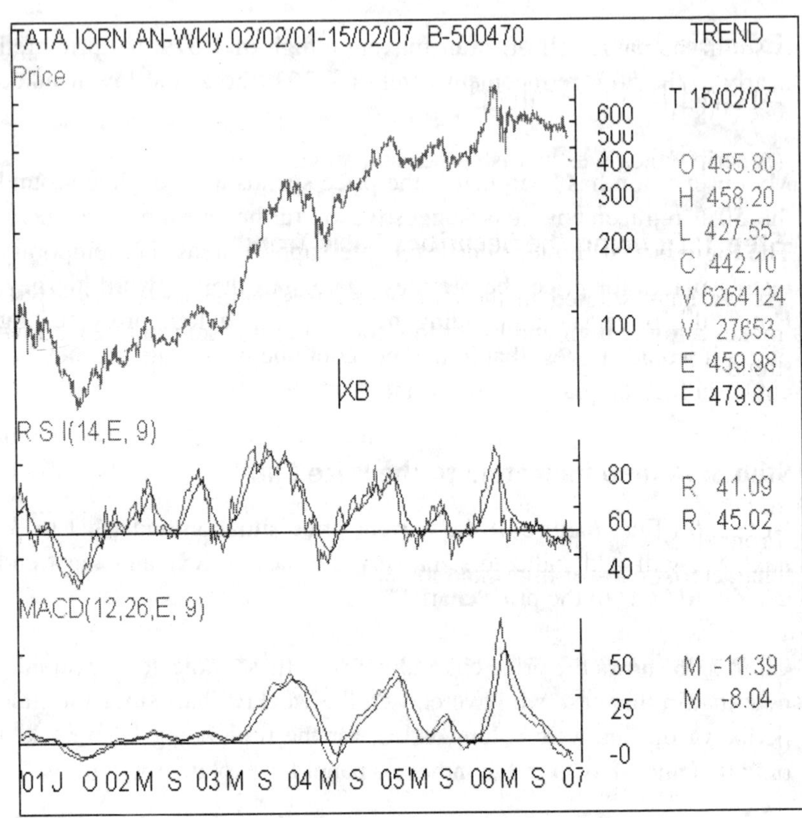

Chart 8.06: **Tisco weekly price chart along with indicators**

Even the MACD which remained above the zero line almost throughout the rally since 2002, has begun showing signs of weakness and is remaining below zero for a longer than usual time.

The strategy in such a case would be to try and exit long position in any 'corrective' price up-moves up to the ₹ 480 – ₹ 500 levels (the 200 DMA being at ₹ 480).

The trader should now become bullish only if prices are able to break the resistance zone of ₹ 521 – ₹ 567.

Example 2

Arvind Mills Limited

(A scrip which was bearish — or in a down trend)

Step 1: Defining the Security's Basic Trend

As we have studied in the earlier chapters, when a security's price makes a lower high and lower low formation it is said to be in a down trend.

In Chart 8.07, we can see that from early 2003 the scrip of Arvind Mills Ltd. was in an up trend which began at ₹ 20 levels. This up trend continued till the prices touched a high of ₹ 144 in mid-2005. From then on the scrip started a down trend — making the characteristic lower highs and lower lows.

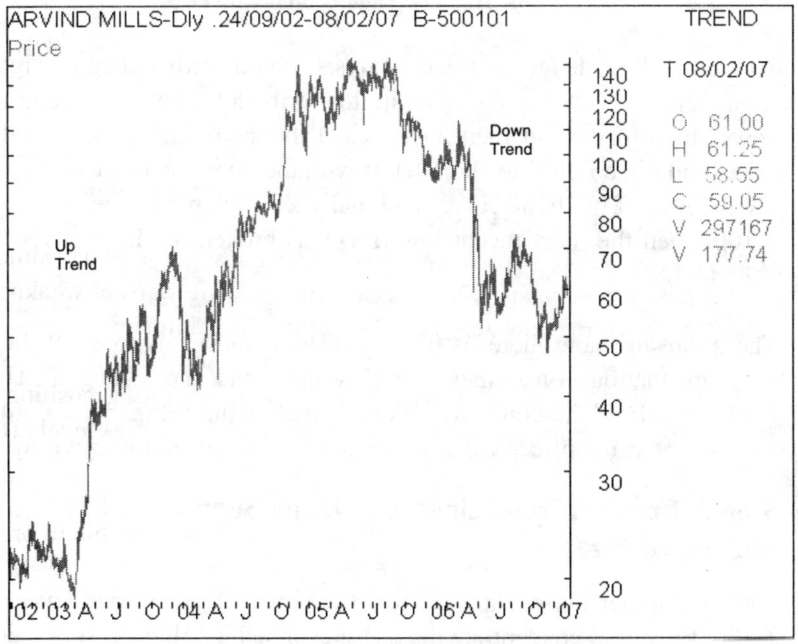

Chart 8.07: **Arvind Mills daily price chart**

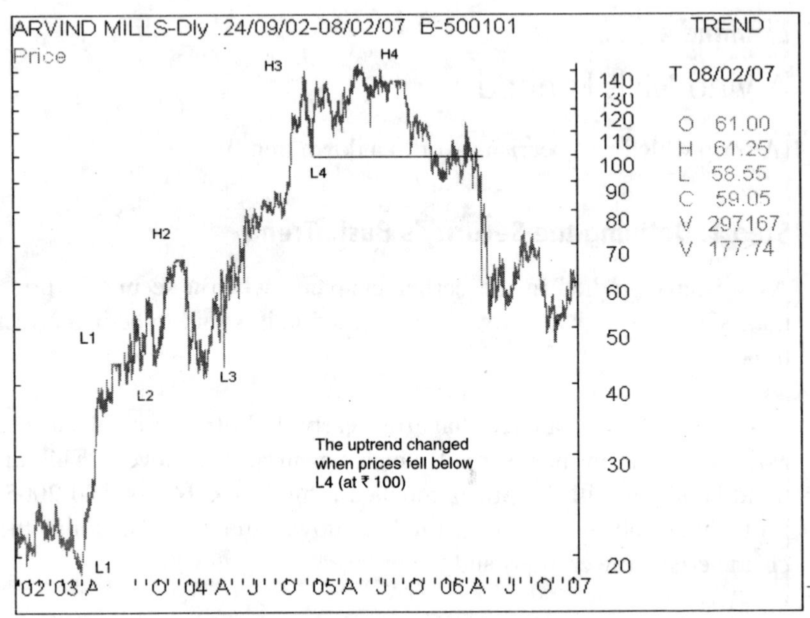

Chart 8.08: **Trend definitions on Arvind Mills**

This basic knowledge of trend analysis would have indicated right from October 2005 that the trend in this scrip had changed from up to down. Investors could then have exited the stock and traders could have used price rallies to short sell it with the intention of buying it at lower levels. This trend reversal signal was available to the trader at ₹ 100 when the most recent low (L4) was broken on the down side (Chart 8.08.).

The point to note here is that investors should ignore all buy recommendations once they see that the trend has changed. The fundamentals of the company would start showing weak signals only subsequently, but prices tell you in advance that something is wrong.

Step 2: Drawing Trend Lines with Major Support and Resistance Areas

Once the trader knows that the trend is down below a price level of ₹ 100, he should concentrate his energies in using rallies to short sell,

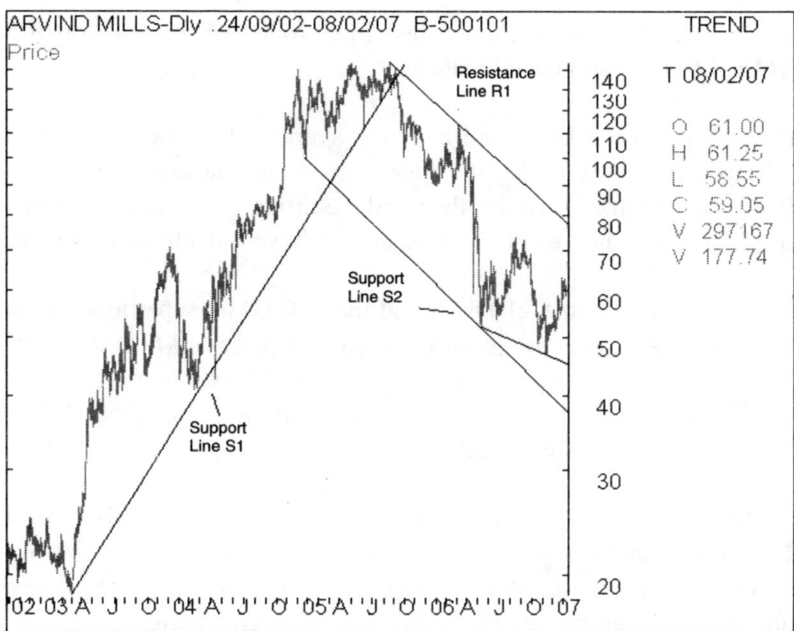

Chart 8.09: **Arvind Mills daily price chart showing support and resistance lines**

or exit any buying position. Also from the lower highs formation, the trader can draw a resistance trend line to get an idea as to the likely future levels where prices will see selling pressure (Resistance line R1 indicated on the top right corner of Chart 8.09).

As of the date of this analysis, such a level where prices were likely to see selling pressure was near ₹ 77 while support was slightly below ₹ 50. This then gives us a sense of the likely price range in the near future.

Step 3: Incorporating Moving Averages on the Price Chart

Having identified the support and resistance trend lines, let's try to validate our analysis by superimposing on the price chart the medium term and long term moving averages. These will confirm whether our trend analysis so far is correct or not.

For this purpose, I have chosen the widely followed combination of 5 DMA, 21 DMA and the 200 DMA.

The shorter term 5 DMA and 21 DMA averages have been chosen to help us make actual trades at a later stage in our analysis. But the 200 DMA, as explained earlier is the trend identifier — if prices are below 200 DMA then the trend is bearish, and if above it the trend is bullish.

Chart 8.10 depicts the 21 DMA and the 200 DMA superimposed on the price chart. You would observe that the price fell below its 200 DMA at ₹ 120 levels giving the investor an early warning of a likely trend change. This was then confirmed when the prices broke below ₹ 100 as we saw in the preceding paragraphs.

At the time of this analysis (8 February 2007), the 200 DMA was at ₹ 66 which can be considered an early signal to investors of a change in the current trend from down to up. This will be confirmed if at a future date the price rises above and makes a higher high.

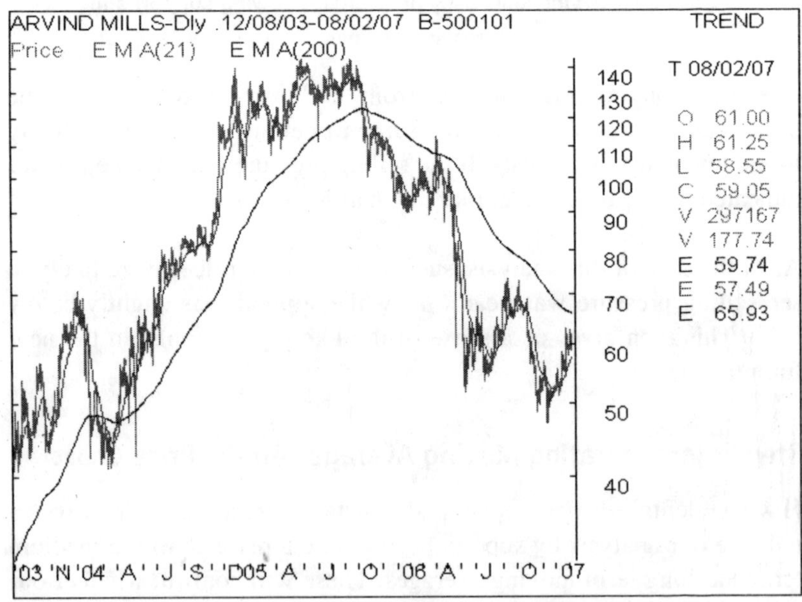

Chart 8.10: **Arvind Mills daily price chart with moving averages**

Step 4: Determining Price Levels Using the Retracement Theory

Readers will recall from Chapter 5 that retracement levels provide us with a rough guide as to the price levels where prices are likely to find resistance in their attempt to move back up.

For this, we need the previous significant high and the previous significant low. In Chart 8.11 we have the significant high of ₹ 144 and the recent significant low reached at ₹ 47.

Now assuming that this low of ₹ 47 will not be breached in the near future, we draw the retracement levels from the high of ₹ 144 to the low of ₹ 47. Chart 8.11 indicates these retracement levels.

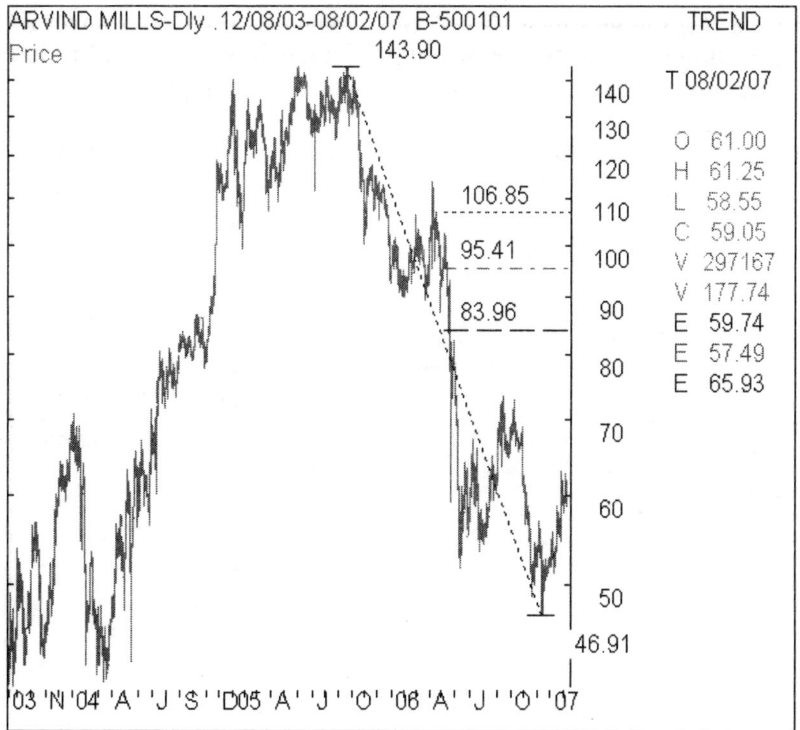

Chart 8.11. **Arvind Mills daily price chart showing retracement levels**

We find that the first retracement level of 38.20% is at ₹ 84, the second or 50% level is at ₹ 95, and the final 61.80% retracement level is at ₹ 106.

These can also be computed manually as explained in Chapter 5.

Step 5: Adding Indicators to the Price Chart

Now for a final picture of the current price situation and what to do next, we add indicators to the price charts — the very volatile stochastic, the slower RSI, and the trend decider MACD.

Chart 8.12 shows the price chart with its three indicators.

Starting from the lowest panel, we find that for most of the duration of the price down move the MACD remained below the zero level suggesting (and confirming) that the trend was weak.

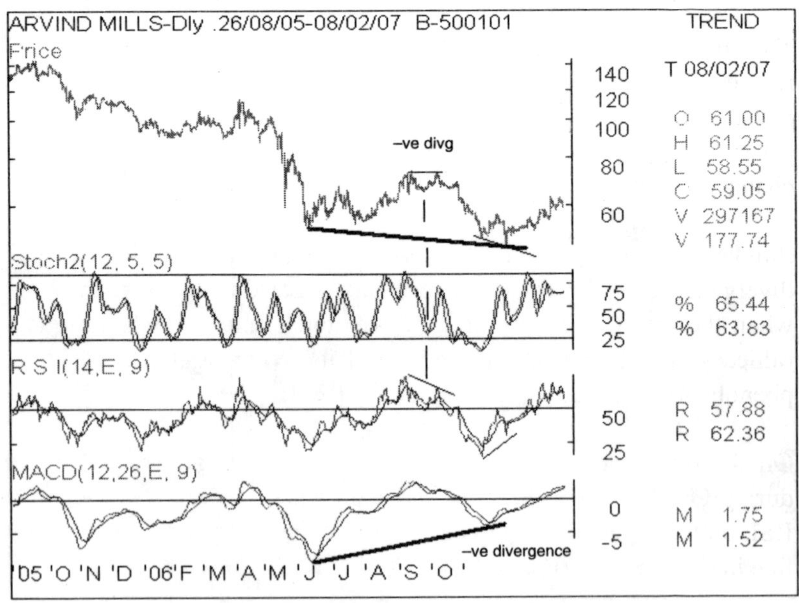

Chart 8.12: **Arvind Mills daily price chart with indicators**

The second last panel shows the RSI. You would observe that the RSI tried to move up above its 50 (mid-point) level but almost always failed to sustain there. Only during the three-month period from August to October 2006 could the RSI maintain above 50 suggesting a positive medium term up move.

The panel just below the price is the volatile stochastic indicator. During the periods when RSI remained below 50, the sell signal on stochastic would have given a short-term trader some good profitable trades. But buy signals may not give good results because the stochastic being a more sensitive oscillator would be more profitable in the direction of the medium term trend as defined by the RSI.

Additional Analysis: Divergence

Let us now look for a divergence, i.e. whether any indicator gave signals contrary to the price move. We find that the trend decider MACD did indeed give a positive divergence — note the thick line drawn on Chart 8.12.

This means that the price then made new lows but the indicator refused to make a newer low. As we learnt earlier this is called a positive divergence and it tells the trader that the recent fall of the price (to its new low of ₹ 47) was a false panic and that a trend change is likely.

Similarly, on the medium term RSI indicator there was a positive divergence (see the thin line in Chart 8.12). Incidentally, this was when the recent new low of ₹ 47 was made, after which the prices rallied such that the RSI value neared its overbought zone of 70, a phenomenon we studied in Chapter 7 on RSI.

On the other hand, you would also observe a negative divergence during October when the price made an equal high at ₹ 73 while the RSI, and also the MACD made a lower high (see the broken vertical line in Chart 8.12.)

Conclusion

In this chapter I have tried to highlight the great value of combining the various tools and techniques of technical analysis which we studied in the earlier chapters. My attempt has been to explain these as simply as possible and at the same time provide you useful insights into the science and art of understanding how prices behave.

Readers who apply this step by step methodology suggested may want to either add some more steps or modify any of the steps mentioned, as they grow more proficient.

As you analyze additional price charts of different types of securities, the underlying process will become clearer. I suggest that beginners in this field must study and analyze as many charts of varied securities as possible before applying this knowledge to trading and investing.

In the next chapter, an attempt is made to provide the reader with analyses of a variety of such securities, including stocks, commodities and indices.

9

Application of Technical Analysis to Stocks, Commodities and Indices

'More people have talent than discipline. That's why discipline pays better.'

– Mike Price

Analysis of Infosys Technologies Ltd.

Analysis of Gold Futures (in US$)

Analysis of Nasdaq Index

Technical analysis can be applied to study the price behavior of any tradable security.

Thus, the principles we have studied apply equally to any price chart — whether it be of a share traded on the Bombay Stock Exchange, or a currency such as the Euro traded on the foreign exchange markets, or any commodity such as gold and silver traded on Nymex, or even the widely tracked international indices such as Dow Jones Index or the Nasdaq.

In this chapter we will analyze three different types of markets. Of course, this is not an exhaustive analysis of the securities mentioned nor is it the only method of analysis.

While the earlier chapter tried to provide a step-by-step framework of approaching a security, in this chapter we will follow the same, or similar steps but without describing the detailed a step-by-step narration.

I have chosen Infosys Technologies as the stock to be analyzed. This is one of the most highly traded stocks in the Indian stock exchanges and is an important part of both Sensex and Nifty — the two widely tracked Indian stock indices.

Second, I have chosen gold as the commodity to be analyzed. Gold is actively traded on the Nymex, and has also found favor on the Indian commodity exchanges.

Thirdly, I have chosen the Nasdaq index which is also a widely tracked index the world over.

It may be pertinent to note that all actively traded shares, derivatives, currencies, and commodities can be analyzed in a similar fashion.

Example 1

Analysis of Infosys Technologies Limited

Before analyzing the daily chart of any share, it is always better to start with its weekly charts, or even the monthly charts. The purpose is to get a perspective of how prices have behaved in the recent past over a longer time frame, and what has been the direction of price movement.

Consider Chart 9.01, the weekly chart of Infosys Technologies along with its crucial indicators like the RSI and MACD.

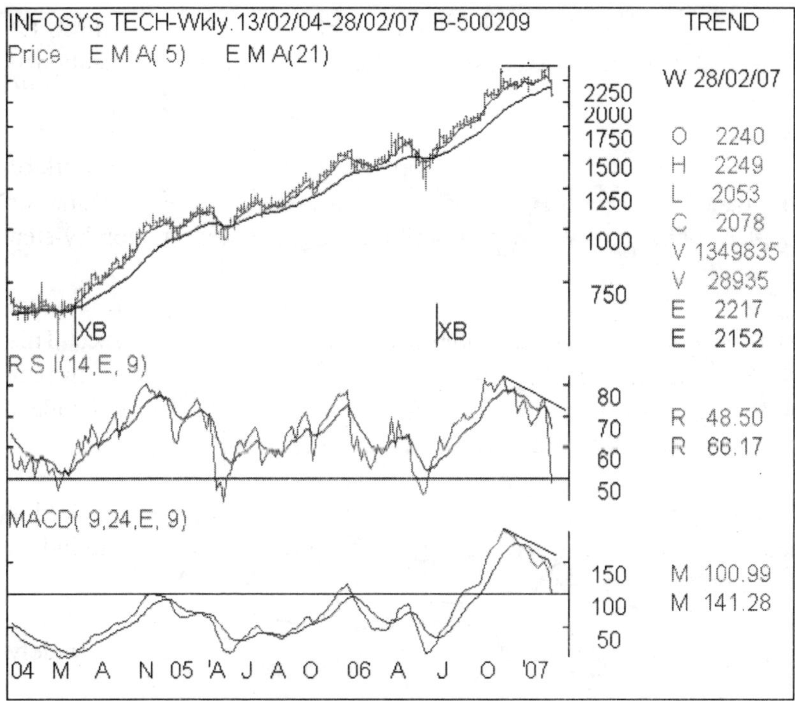

Chart 9.01: **Weekly chart of Infosys Technologies Ltd.**

The weekly chart indicates that the overall trend of the scrip has been up during the period under study. This can also be gathered from the fact that during the entire run up from the sub-₹ 700 levels to the high of ₹ 2,400 in February 2007, the RSI more or less remained above its crucial mid-point of 50.

However, an element of exhaustion in prices can be seen at the beginning of 2007 as the indicators and the price, which were earlier in tandem, began showing signs of fatigue.

This is corroborated by a negative divergence on both the weekly RSI as well as the weekly MACD. While the price made a newer high, the indicators failed to do so. Thus, the higher time frame price chart is suggesting to the trader to be cautious when trading on the upside based on the daily charts.

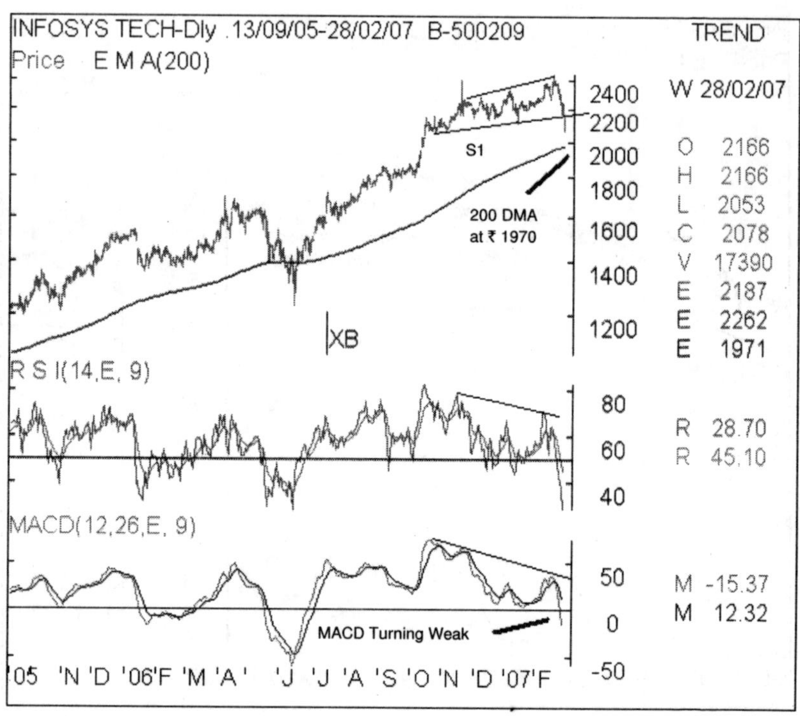

Chart 9.02: **Daily chart of Infosys Technologies Ltd.**

Based on this broader picture let us now review the daily price chart along with indicators and the 200 DMA (Chart 9.02).

The recent sell-off led to the price breaking below the immediate support line (marked S1) which had provided support to the price since October 2006.

There is a negative divergence both on the RSI and the MACD. This is the similar to what we saw on the weekly chart (Chart 9.01). Only, it's more prominent on the daily chart.

Also, the immediate support level for the stock is the 200 DMA which presently is at ₹ 1,970. This, therefore, gives the trader a short term level for profit booking on his short sell trade.

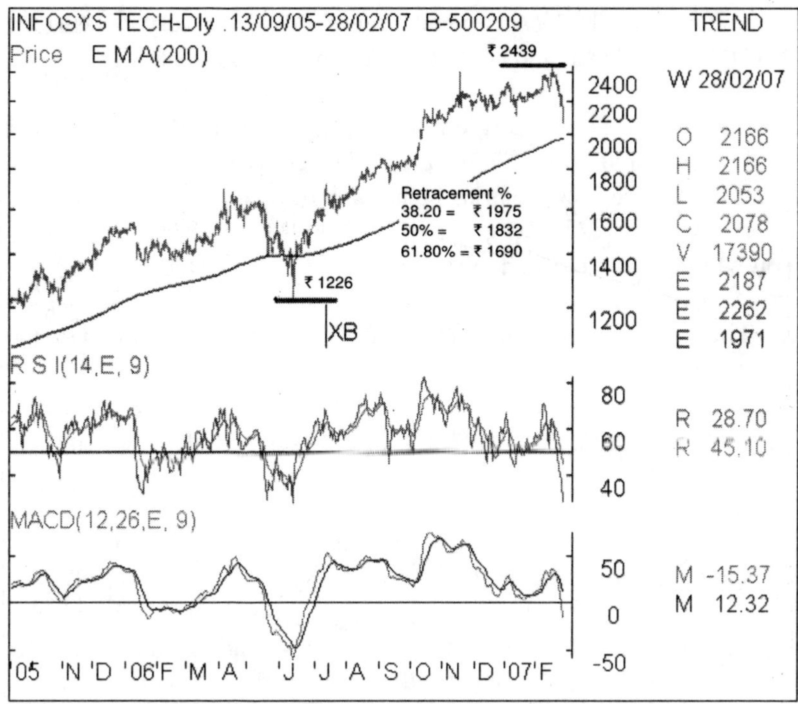

Chart 9.03: **Infosys with its retracement levels**

Another observation which should make the trader (and now the investor, too) cautious is that the MACD has fallen below the zero line after about ten months. This is suggestive of weakness.

Let us now analyze the daily chart based on the retracement levels to get an idea of the areas where we can expect the price to get support during its downward journey (Chart 9.03).

The most recent low for calculating the retracement level is the May-June 2006 period, when prices fell to a low of ₹ 1,226. Thereafter the price almost doubled and touched a high of ₹ 2,440.

Now since the prices are in a falling mode, we compute the retracement levels which are at ₹ 1,975, ₹ 1,832 and ₹ 1,690 levels, corresponding to 38.20%, 50% and 61.80%, respectively.

Incidentally, the first retracement level of ₹ 1,975 is very close to the 200 DMA of ₹ 1,970 and could therefore be an important level.

The last important support for the stock based on the retracement theory is ₹ 1,690 (say, ₹ 1,700). It will therefore be important for a trader to observe how the price behaves in the ₹ 1,700 price area.

You will note that in this analysis we've:

1. Tried to understand the share's price behavior in relation to the past price move;

2. Concluded that the current trend is weakening based on the divergences;

3. Identified the price levels where a trader can book profits on his short sell position; and

4. Suggested that the longer term investor should be cautious of his investment and, at least partially, book profit or hedge himself.

Example 2

Analysis of Gold Futures on Nymex (in US$)

Consider Chart 9.04 of gold futures quoted in US $ traded on Nymex.

The weekly chart suggests that the overall upward trend of gold futures remained intact till early 2007. Also, the weekly RSI is above 50, and the weekly MACD is above the zero line and in a rising mode, suggesting bullishness in the medium to long term.

You will observe that the weekly RSI and the price gave similar breakouts on the upside.

Now let us review the daily chart to get some further insights into the price levels (Chart 9.05).

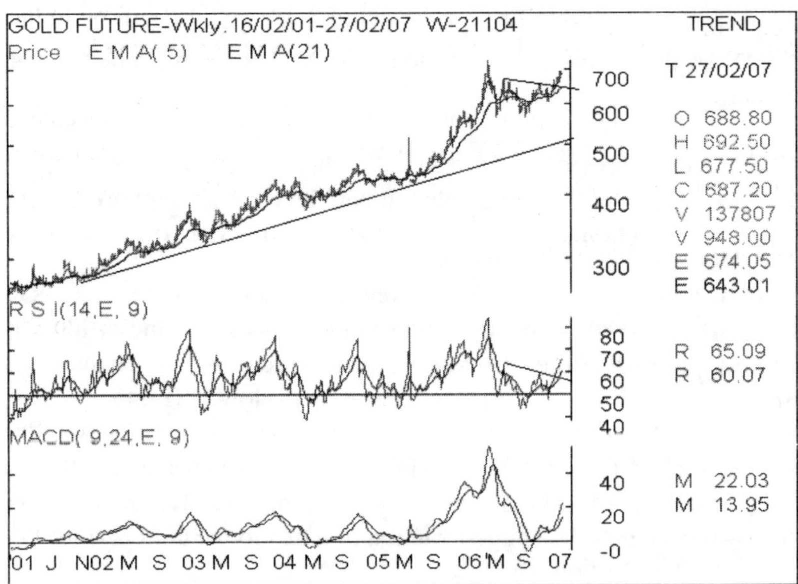

Chart 9.04: **Weekly chart on Nymex of Gold Futures.**

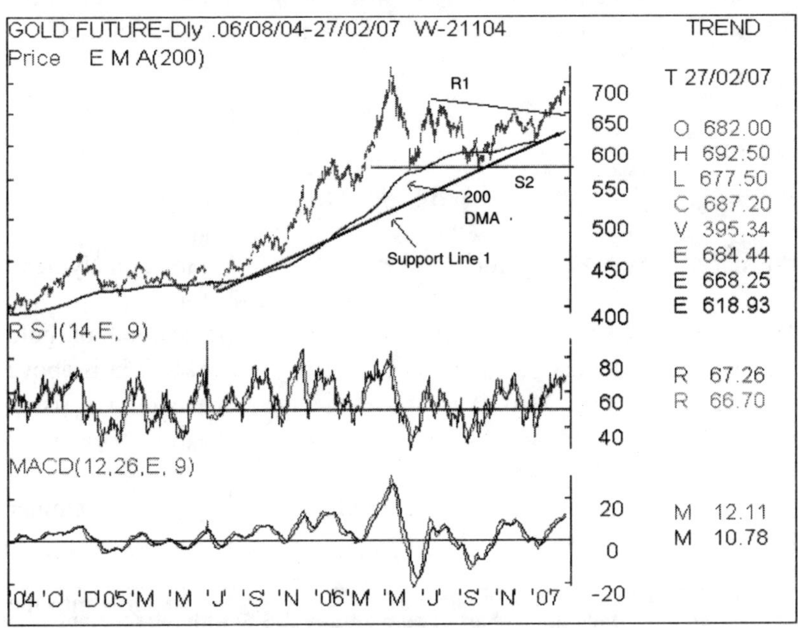

Chart 9.05: **Daily chart of gold futures along with its indicators and 200 DMA**

You will observe from Chart 9.05 that the price remained above its 200 DMA during the current up move. In fact, it seems to be finding support there.

Also, the medium term support line (the thick line marked as 'support line 1') defines the intermediate support level. This support line as well as the 200 DMA provide support at around US$ 610.

Secondly, the price has lately broken above the resistance line R1. Thus, in any corrective down move, this resistance line will be a support provider (refer to role reversal discussed in Chapter 2). Accordingly, the support price level is at just below US$ 645.

The daily chart (Chart 9.06) also provides positive cues as the RSI is above 50 and MACD above zero and, importantly, there is no divergence in either to suggest caution or a halt to the current trend.

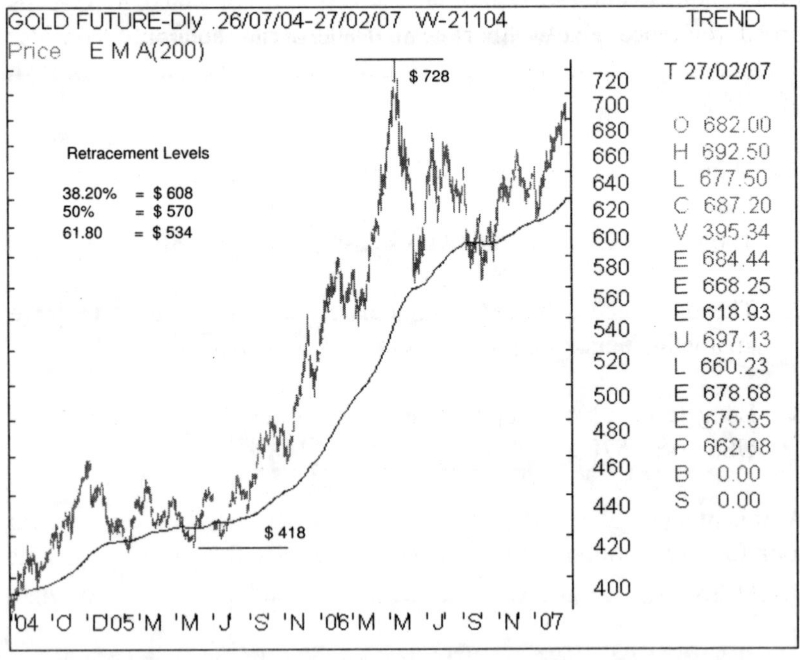

Chart 9.06: **Daily price chart of gold futures (US $) with retracement levels**

Now let us see whether the price levels identified above are further confirmed by the retracement theory.

The most recent important low can be taken at US$ 418, from where the rally started its move. We compute retracement levels taking this low of US$ 418 and the high of US$ 728. The retracement levels are indicated in Chart 9.06.

You will observe that the first retracement level of US$ 608 is again very close to the 200 DMA and the intermediate support line indicated in Chart 9.05. This further strengthens the validity of a crucial price support area for the security around US$ 610.

Similarly, the second retracement level of US$ 570 is quite close to the price support line; marked S2 in Chart 9.05.

Please note that these retracement levels are computed to give us broad reference levels. Short term traders can no doubt consider retracement levels from the low of US$ 560 and the subsequent high of US$ 684.

The above analysis therefore provides us the following perspective:

1. The weekly chart of gold futures is suggesting a bullish trend.

2. The daily chart indicates immediate support at US$ 645 price area while major support exists at US$ 610 price area.

3. Long term major support may be considered in the vicinity of US$ 560 – 570.

At this juncture, therefore, a trader and investor in gold futures should look for buying opportunities whenever the price falls, rather than exit his positions.

Example 3

Analysis of Nasdaq Index

Let us consider the weekly chart of Nasdaq (Chart 9.07).

We observe that the Nasdaq index has been in an up trend since mid-2003 and, lately, it has been in a rising channel. The support line of the channel is at 2,100 points.

There is, however, an indication of caution on the weekly charts in the form of a negative divergence on both RSI and the MACD. This suggests that traders may book profits on their current long positions and wait for the RSI value to fall below into the oversold zone.

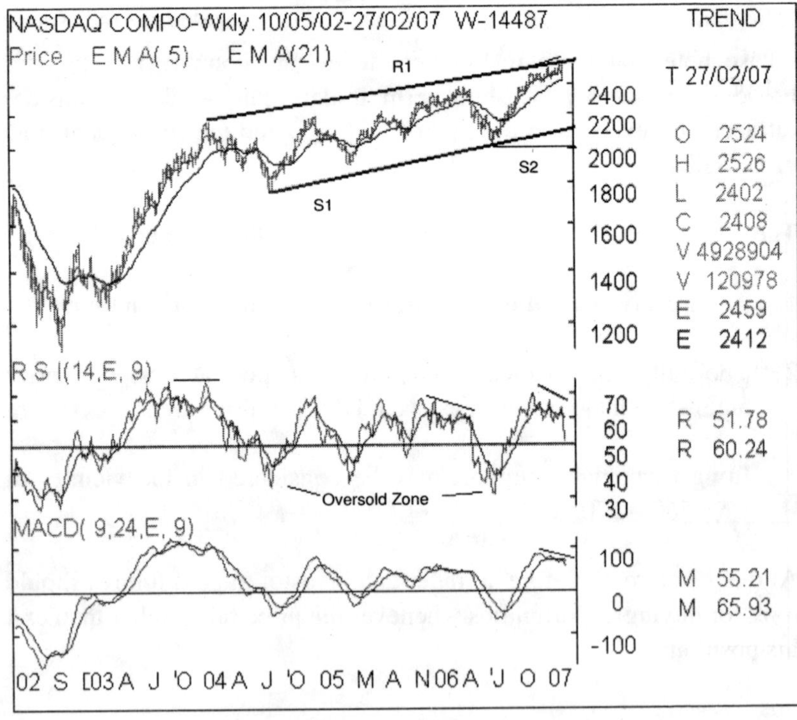

Chart 9.07: **Weekly chart of Nasdaq along with its indicators**

You may have noted that the negative divergence on RSI on two earlier occasions had led to the RSI values subsequently falling into the oversold zone, once in mid-2004 and again in mid-2006 (please refer to markings on Chart 9.07).

It is therefore likely that the index would fall to the support level of 2,100 points by which time the RSI would also test the oversold zone.

The subsequent important support for the Nasdaq below 2,100 is at 2,000 (marked as S2 on Chart 9.07) which is also its most recent low.

Now let us view the daily chart to get a closer look at our analysis of the Nasdaq (Chart 9.08).

The daily chart confirms the cautionary note provided by the weekly chart. There is a clearly visible negative divergence on the RSI. The MACD, too, is quite near to the crucial zero line.

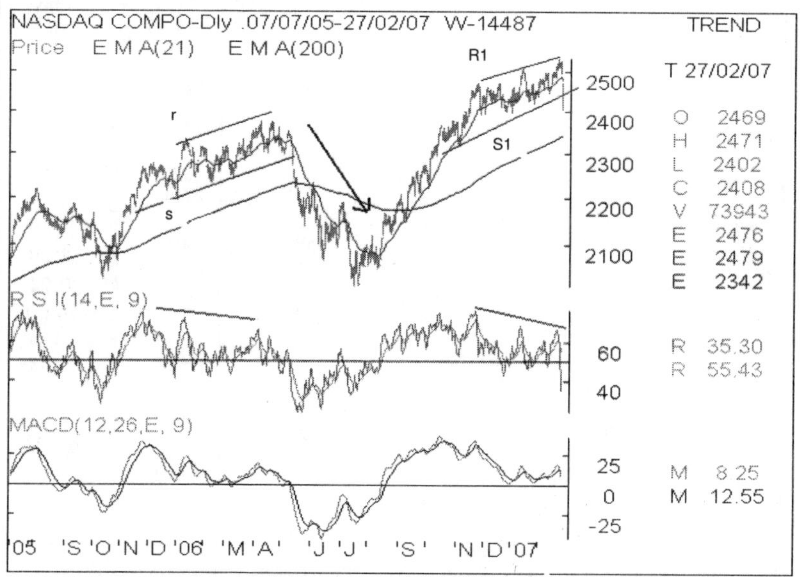

Chart 9.08: **Daily chart of Nasdaq along with indicators and 200 DMA**

Moreover, the short term support line of S1 has been broken. You will also observe that the latest price formation is similar to the one formed in early 2006 which was followed by a fall in mid-2006 (one more proof that 'history repeats'!). Please see the price movement following the markings 'r' and 's' on Chart 9.08.

The immediate support level is the crucial 200 DMA which stands at 2,350.

Let's now move on to the retracement analysis (Chart 9.09).

The price up move from the May 2006 low of 2,012 to the latest high of 2,531, is likely to find support in a corrective down move, initially at 2,333 points (38.20% retracement), then at 2,272 points (50% retracement) and then, importantly, at 2,210 (61.80% retracement).

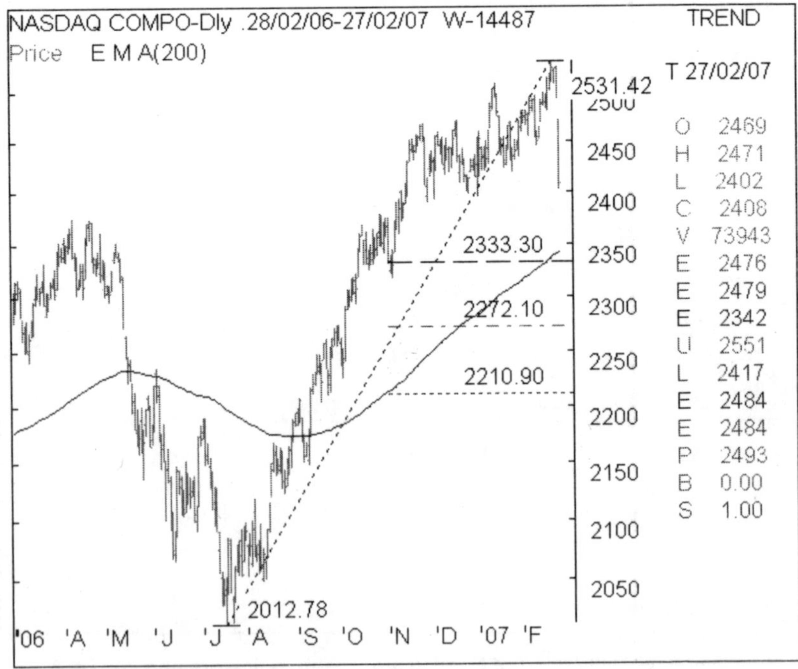

Chart 9.09: **Daily price chart of Nasdaq along with retracement levels**

You would already have observed that the 38.20% retracement of 2,333 is very near to the crucial 200 DMA of 2,350, thus making it an important price level to watch.

Moreover, you would also have noted that the 61.80% retracement level of 2,110 is very near to the weekly lower channel support level of 2,100. Thus, this too could be a crucial trend-decider in the future. Any break below this 2,100 level could be damaging to the ongoing up trend.

10

Technical Analysis for the Long Term Investor

'We are all apprentices in a craft where no one ever becomes a master.'

– Ernest Hemingway

Trend Analysis on a Higher Time Frame

200 DMA: The Trend Decider

Long Term Moving Average Crossovers — 50 DMA and 200 DMA

Monthly RSI as a Long Term Trend Identifier

One of the major criticisms leveled against the use of price charts is that these are merely a trader's tools, and do not offer much benefit to long term investors. Most proponents of fundamental analysis have an inherent dislike for technical analysis, though they do not speak against it as openly as they used to few years ago.

These two approaches of analyzing a security are not mutually exclusive and, in fact, can be used in a manner that is complementary to each other.

There are various technical tools and trend analysis techniques which can be of immense help even to a long term investor.

In fact, when fundamental analysis is coupled with even a working knowledge of technical analysis, it can lead to a very comprehensive analysis of a security. Moreover, technical analysis can assist investors in timing their purchase and sales of securities more judiciously.

For the long term investor, a knowledge of trends along with moving averages and certain key indicators would help in validating a security's fundamentals. **However, in an important deviation from what we have studied in the preceding chapters, a long term investor should use the higher time frame**. Thus while a short and medium term trader would use daily or weekly charts for trend identification and entering / exiting trades, the long term investor should give more emphasis to the weekly, monthly and, even, quarterly charts.

There is a relatively complex branch of technical analysis known as the Elliot Wave Theory which too analyses securities from a longer term perspective. This branch is beyond the scope of this book. However, even basic technical analysis covered in this book has the potential to provide supportive analysis to long term investing.

My own use of technical analysis for long term investing comprises:

1. Trend analysis on a higher time frame;

2. 200 DMA;

3. Long term moving average crossovers (50 / 200); and

4. The monthly RSI.

Trend Analysis on a Higher Time Frame

We now shift from daily charts to the higher time frame monthly charts, since a long term investor is interested in basic long term trend rather than the day-to-day price fluctuations.

Let us consider the monthly chart of Zee Telefilms Limited (Chart 10.01).

You would observe that since the technology stock meltdown in mid-2000, the scrip remained in a down trend and even touched the sub-₹ 70 levels.

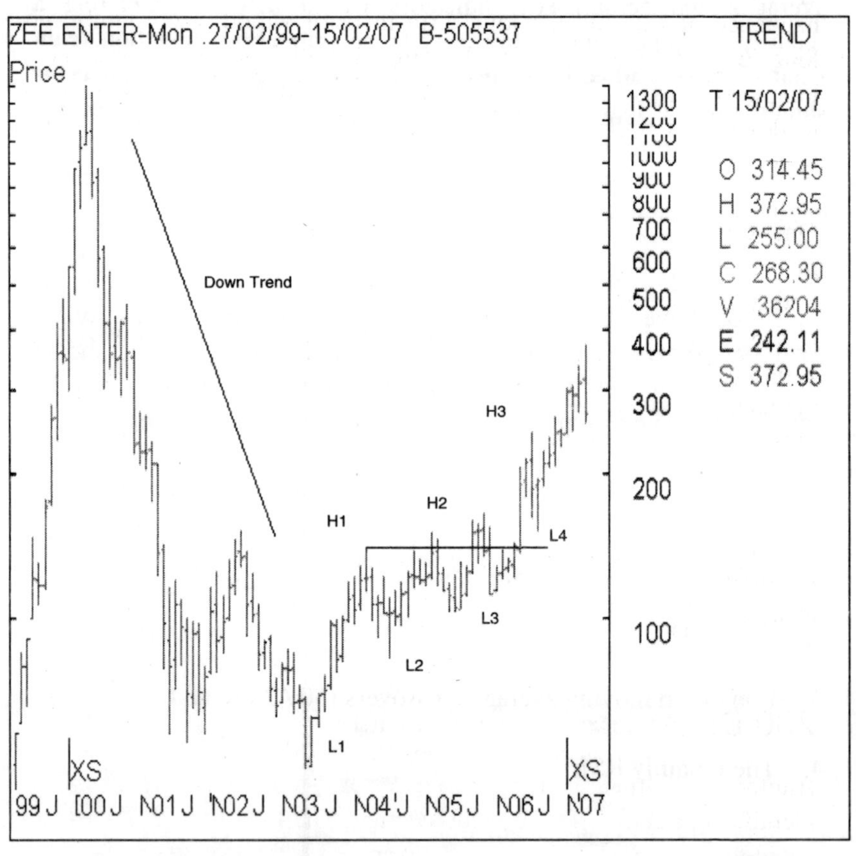

Chart 10.01: **Identification of trend change on the monthly chart of Zee Telefilms**

The sub-₹ 70 low level is marked on Chart 10.01 as L1. The subsequent high of ₹ 155 is marked as H1, followed by a higher low formation at L2.

The basic trend will be considered as having changed from down to up when the price rose above ₹ 155, after the low of L2. This happened at H2, and the long term investor would, accordingly, go long (buy) the stock at ₹ 155 keeping an initial stop loss at L2. This long position will continue until the primary long term trend changes to down at a future date — which could be some months or years later.

One important point I would like to make here is that most long term investors have a false notion that stop loss is a concept meant only for traders and speculators. By not using a stop loss, long term investors risk holding a stock, or worse, adding to their holding all the way into a down trend. They would typically track the fundamentals of a company at most every quarter, only to find that price had already outstripped the fundamentals.

An informed and enlightened investor is one who respects the market's verdict of price. This sort of informed decision is best possible only when fundamental analysis is combined with technical analysis, taking advantage of both.

200 DMA: The Trend Decider

Another tool which the long term investor can use very effectively for identifying trends is the moving average. The long term 200 DMA is a widely used and reliable moving average for this purpose.

However, medium term investors can also use 100 DMA if their investment time frame is lower at, say, 6 to 9 months.

Chart 10.02: **Sensex above its 200 DMA**

Consider the daily chart of the Sensex (Chart 10.02).

In Chart 10.02 you would observe that the Sensex rose above its 200 DMA in this daily chart, which was then at 3,600 level, in the second quarter of 2003. After that the price did not fall below its 200 DMA till the May 2004 crash when there was a change of government due to the general elections. The Sensex gave a sell then at the 5,500 level, only to go back above its 200 DMA at 5,700 level. This buy signal remained valid till the 10,000 level which was breached in May 2006 following the global commodity and stock market meltdown. The market again recovered and went above its 200 DMA at 10,500 level and reached a higher level of 14,500+ in mid-February 2007.

If one were to discount the small brokerage losses of exiting and re-entering the market in May 2004 and May 2006, a long term investor who followed the buy and sell cues would have profited from the entire rally from 3,500 right up to the 14,500 Sensex level!

Most Sensex stocks also saw similar price moves when looked at through the 200 DMA tool. I strongly suggest the use of 200 DMA by long term investors in every market — stocks, derivatives, commodities, forex, *et al.*

Please also refer to 'Using the magnate characteristic of 200 DMA' in Chapter 4.

Long Term Moving Average Crossovers — 50 DMA and 200 DMA

A logical extension of the 200 DMA tool is the two moving average crossover signal using longer term time periods.

One combination which is both useful and widely followed is the 50 DMA and 200 DMA crossovers.

Let us consider Chart 10.03 of Reliance Capital depicting its 50 DMA and 200 DMA crossovers.

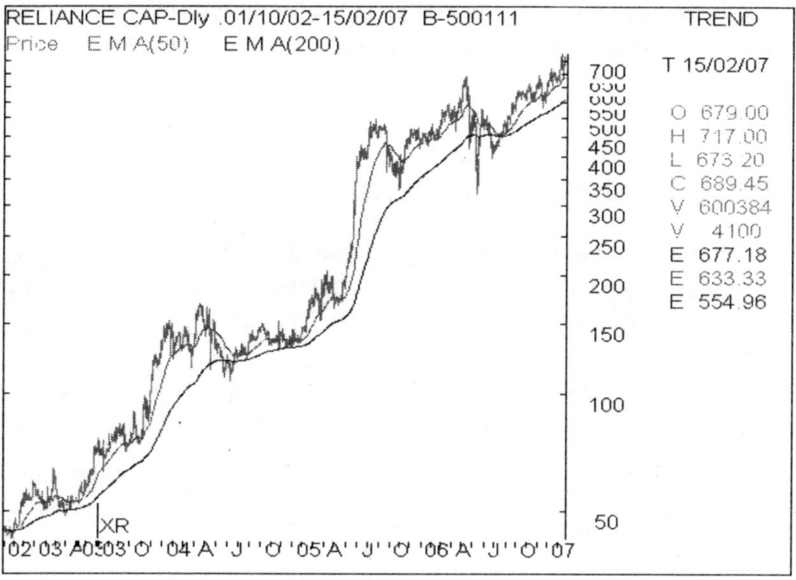

Chart 10.03. **Crossover of two longer term moving averages in Reliance Capital.**

You will observe that the 50 DMA crossed the 200 DMA from below as early as end-2002 at a price of ₹ 40. Thereafter, the 50 DMA remained above the 200 DMA, i.e. in a buy mode, till the end of this chart in February 2007, by when the price had reached close to ₹ 700.

No doubt there will always be fluctuations and corrections in between caused by intermediate trends but an investor following this system must believe in it and hold on to his position so long as the moving averages are in a buy mode. This is actually where the discipline attribute of a trader or an investor comes into play — something which is, frankly, quite difficult to master.

Typically in a system based on longer term time periods, the buy and sell signals generated will not only be slow but it may take some time for the price to negate its previous signal. Thus, a scrip which is in a buy mode in this system will require a larger price more and a longer time to provide a sell signal.

Also, as indicated in Chapter 4, this sort of a system may give some losses if the market is non-trending (range bound) for a longer time period.

Monthly RSI as a Long Term Trend Identifier

Continuing our use of a higher time frame for long term investing (and disinvesting), it is also possible to extend the trend-identification feature of the RSI which was discussed in Chapter 7.

The basic premise was that whenever the RSI value is above its mid-point value of 50 (of its range from 0 and 100), the underlying trend of the security is bullish or positive, and whenever it is below the mid-point value of 50, the trend is held to be bearish or negative. This was described with the help of examples on the daily chart.

Extending the same premise, it has been observed that for long term trend identification purpose, as also for actual entry into and exit from a security, the RSI plotted using a monthly price chart gives fairly reliable signals. Moreover, being 'faster' than the MACD, it tends to give early / advance signal to the investor.

Let us consider Chart 10.04, which is the monthly chart of Sensex. You would observe that since mid-2000 (point 'a' marked on the chart), the RSI was in sell mode (i.e., below its mid-point value of 50) indicating bearishness. This bearish mode extended till early 2003 (point 'b' marked on the chart) when it again gave a buy signal as the RSI value rose above its mid-point value of 50.

You will also note that the RSI remained in buy mode from then on till the date of the chart (mid-February 2007). Thereafter, it moved near to the overbought zone of 75+ RSI value.

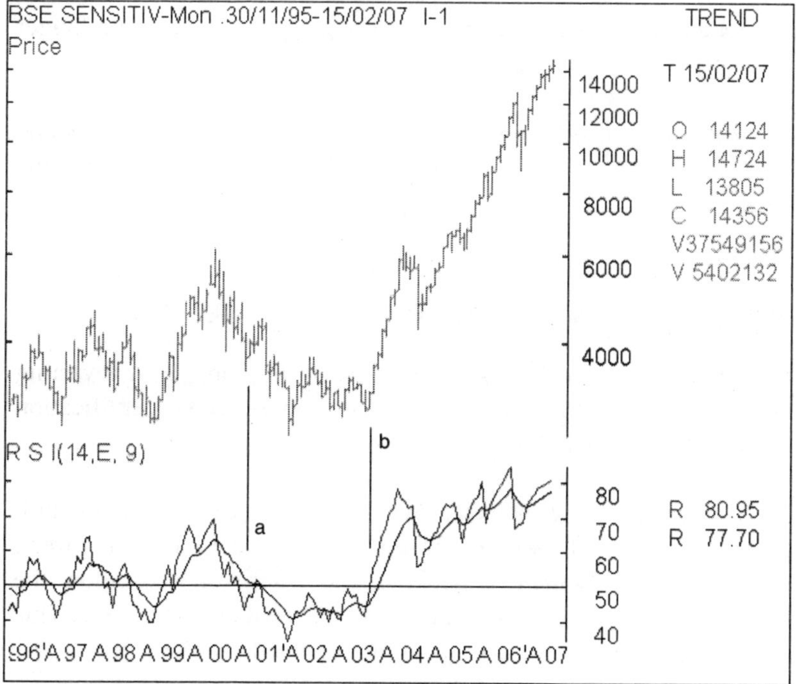

Chart 10.04: **Monthly chart of Sensex RSI was in sell mode from Point a to Point b, and thereafter gave a buy signal**

Even before 2000, despite some hiccups, the RSI mid-point remained a reliable reference for the long term investor on whether to remain in the security or out of it.

This observation is also valid for individual securities.

11

Introduction to Japanese Candlesticks

'In this market, the bulls make money, bears make money but the pigs get slaughtered!'

– Anonymous

The Meaning and Types of Candles

Basic Candlestick Price Patterns

Price charting is usually assumed to be a Western innovation. Financial markets, however, have been known to exist all over the world in varying degrees of development. The early Japanese traders had invented their own method of visually depicting day-to-day price movements, mainly for trading commodities.

Instead of the traditional charts which show a day's open, high, low and close prices in the form of bars, Japanese traders used to plot the same set of data more pictorially — in the form of candles. The major advantage of candlesticks for a user of price charts is that they are more graphically suggestive of the price action of the day. Thus, while a bar on a traditional bar chart may not 'tell' you visually whether the market was bullish or bearish on a particular day, the candlesticks have this feature embedded in them.

The Meaning and Types of Candles

There are mainly three basic types of candles:

1. Bullish candle — also referred to as the white candle;
2. Bearish candle — also referred to as the black candle; and
3. Doji candle.

Let us now look at each of these.

The Bullish Candle (White Candle)

The bullish candle, or white candle, will be formed on a day when the price closes higher than the day's opening price, suggesting that the market is positive. This is plotted as shown in Chart 11.01.

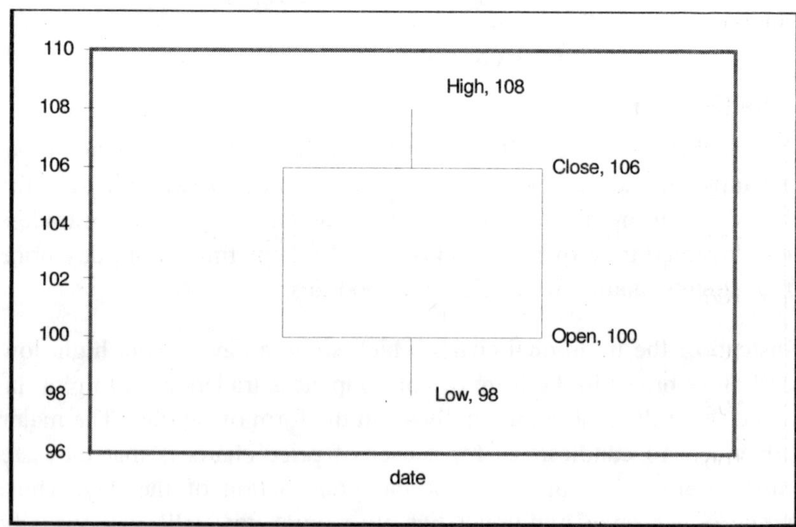

Chart 11.01: **Bullish candle (White candle)**

The Bearish Candle (Black Candle)

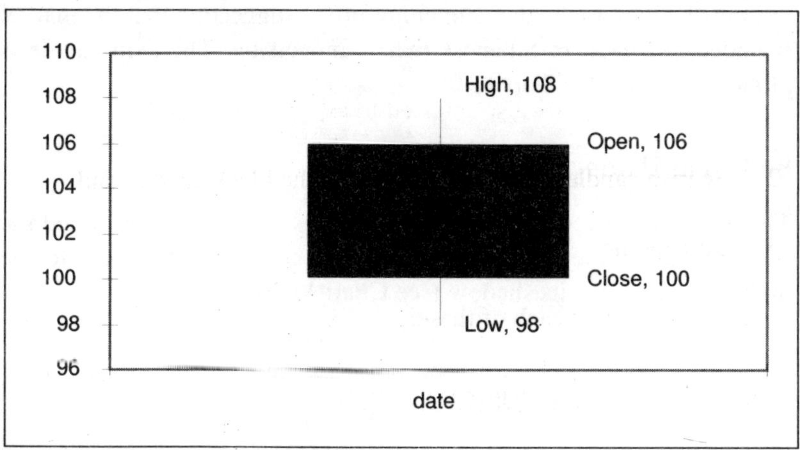

Chart 11.02: **Bearish candle (Black candle)**

The bearish candle, or black candle, is formed on a day when the price closes lower than the day's opening price, suggesting that the market is weak. This is plotted as shown in Chart 11.02.

The Doji Candle

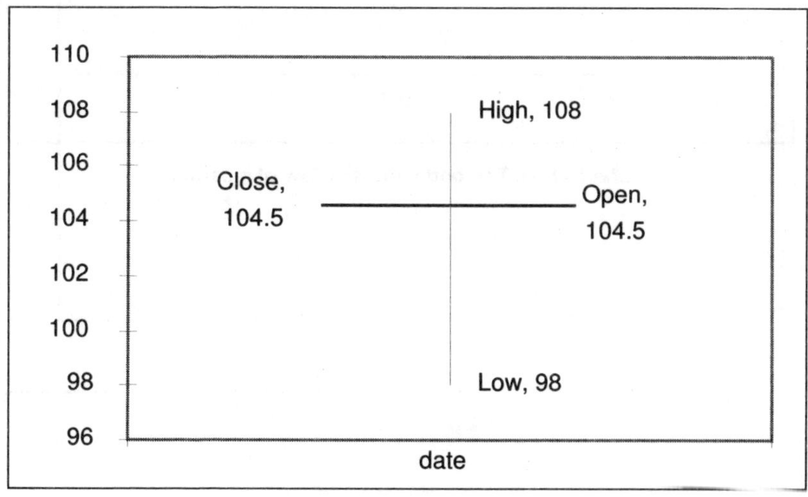

Chart 11.03: **Doji candle**

The Doji candle is formed on a day when the price closes either equal, or almost equal, to the day's opening price, suggesting that the market is undecided. Doji in Japanese means indecision. The Doji candle is plotted as shown in Chart 11.03.

Body and Shadow of the Candle

The distance between the open and the close of a candle is called the body of the candle, while the distance from the open (close) to the high (low) is called its shadow (see Chart 11.04).

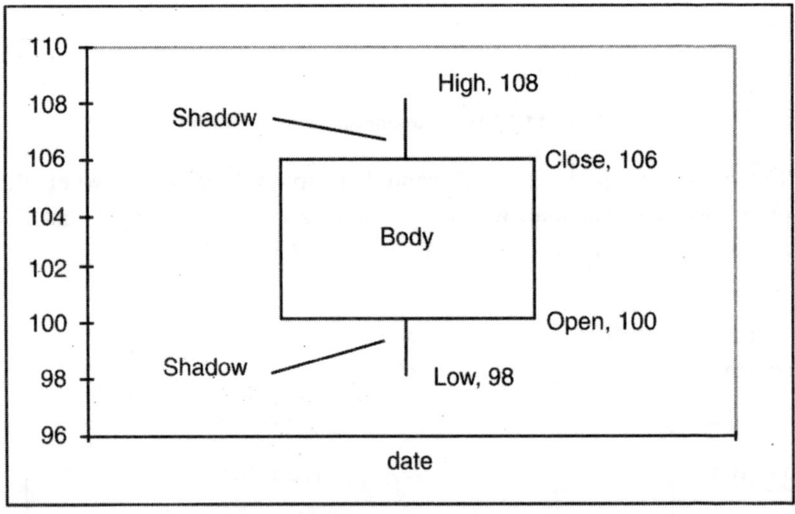

Chart 11.04: **The body and shadow of a candle**

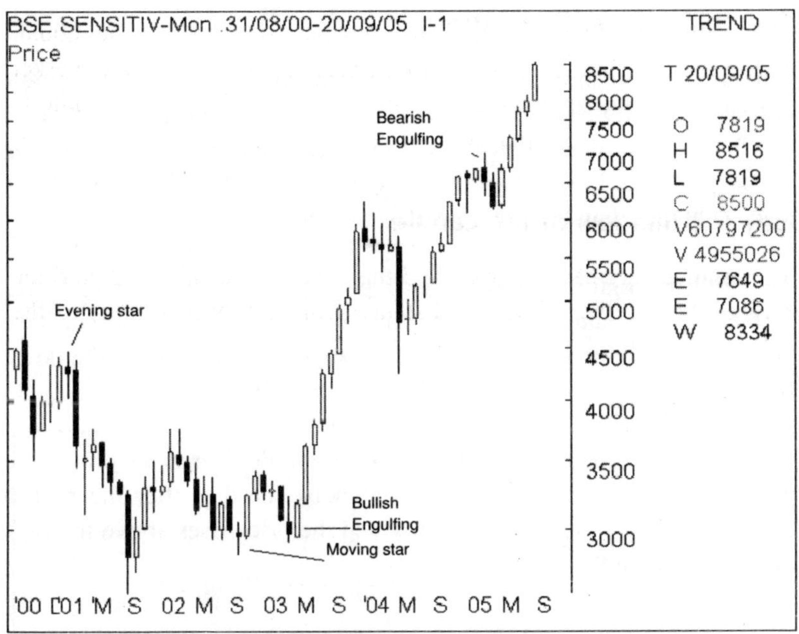

Chart 11.05: **Monthly Sensex chart showing the various types of candlestick and patterns**

Chart 11.05 of Sensex depicts the various types of candlestick and patterns.

Basic Candlestick Price Patterns

As in the case of all price charts used in technical analysis, the major purpose of candlestick charts is to understand market behavior as depicted by the candlestick patterns. These patterns are both easy to understand and, often, visually quite self-evident.

The Bullish Engulfing Pattern

This is a two-candle pattern where the latest day's white candle entirely 'engulfs', i.e. is larger than the body of the previous day's candle. It is formed when the current day's opening price (day 2 in Chart 11.06) is lower than the previous day's close but the closing price is higher than the previous day's open.

The bullish engulfing pattern is a potential bullish reversal signal formed by the latest two days' price move when the markets have been previously in a down trend. It is suggestive of a halt of the down trend which is why it is called the bullish engulfing pattern.

Using the filtering approach for entering a trade, it may be prudent to go long (buy) on the third day — namely, the day after the bullish engulfing pattern is formed — provided the price rises above the high of the white candle.

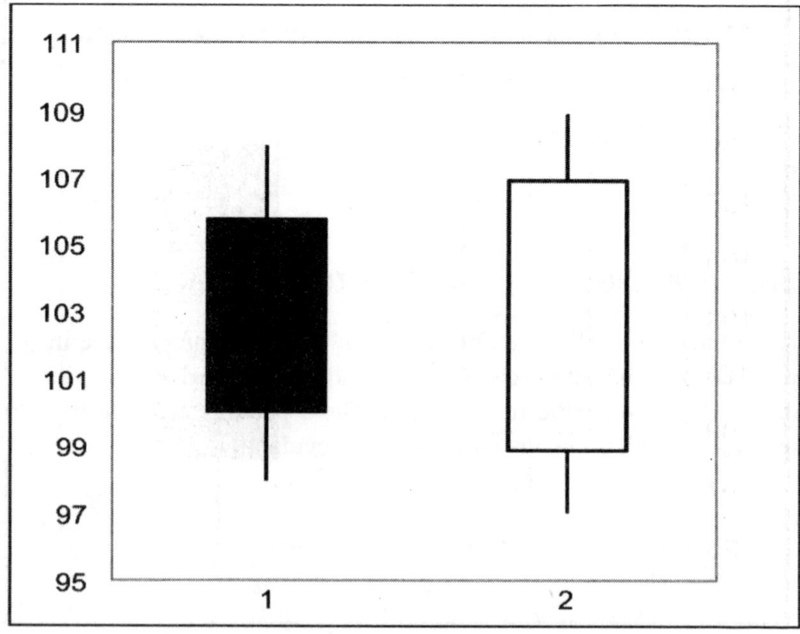

Chart 11.06: **The bullish engulfing pattern**

The Bearish Engulfing Pattern

This is another two-candle pattern and is formed when the current day's black candle entirely 'engulfs' (is larger than) the body of the previous day's candle. It is formed when the current day's price (day 2 in Chart 11.07) opens higher than the previous day's close, and also closes lower than the previous day's close

Usually, the bearish engulfing pattern is formed when the markets have previously been in an up trend. It is suggestive of a halt of the ongoing rally and is a potential bearish reversal signal. Which is why it is called the bearish engulfing pattern.

Using the filtering approach for entering a trade, it may be prudent to go short (sell) the day after the bearish engulfing pattern is formed, and if the price falls below the low of the black candle.

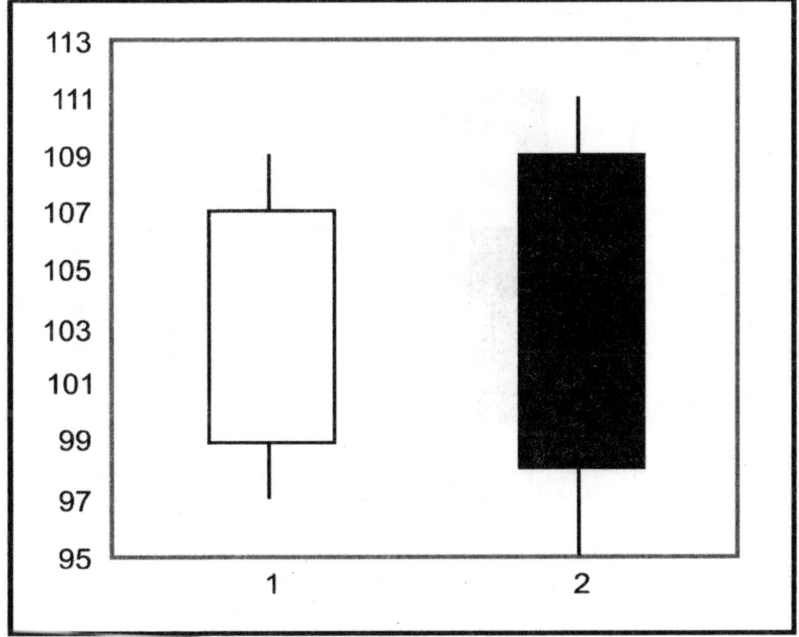

Chart 11.07: **The bearish engulfing pattern**

The Piercing Pattern

This two-candle pattern develops when the latest day's white candle closes above the mid-point of the body of the previous day's black candle. In other words, the piercing pattern is formed when the latest day's opening price (day 2 in Chart 11.08) is lower than the previous day's closing price and also closes above the mid-point of the previous day's black body.

Though not as strong as the bullish engulfing pattern, this pattern also suggests a halt in a down trend. Moreover for entering the trade, it will be prudent to go long (using the filtering approach) though after the scrip crosses the high of the two days.

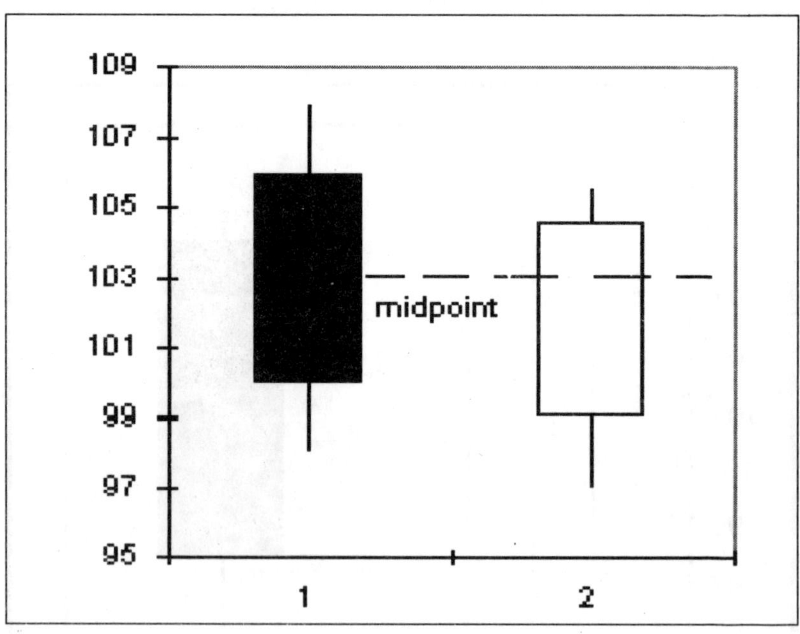

Chart 11.08: **The piercing pattern**

The Dark Cloud Cover Pattern

This pattern is the converse of the piercing pattern and develops when the latest day's black candle closes below the mid-point of the previous day's white candle (Chart 11.09).

It is formed when on the latest day (day 2 in Chart 11.09), the price opens higher than the previous day's close and also closes lower than the mid-point of previous day's white body.

Though not as strong as the bearish engulfing pattern, this pattern also suggests a halt in an up trend. Moreover for entering a trade, it will be prudent to go short (sell) (using the filtering approach) after the scrip falls below the low of the two days.

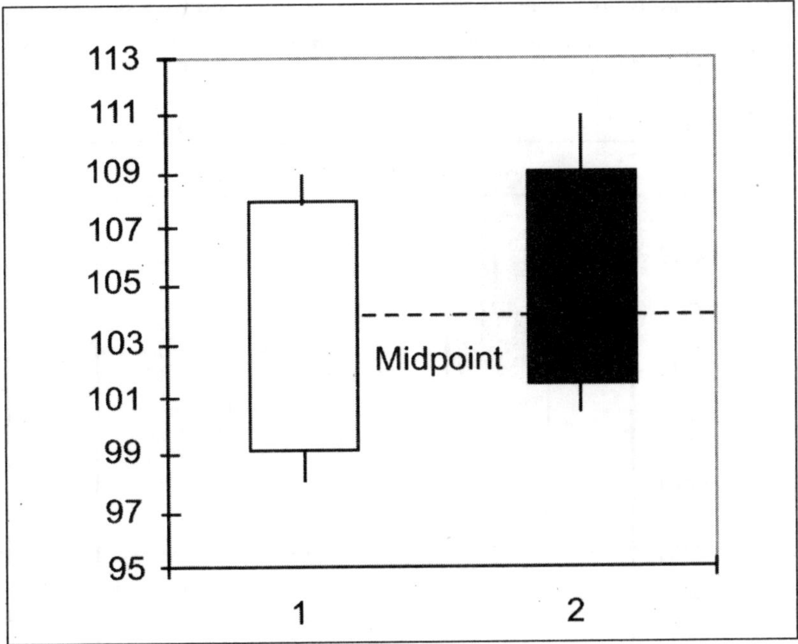

Chart 11.09: **The dark cloud cover pattern**

The Harami (pronounced as 'Haa raa mee') Pattern

Like the previous patterns, this again is a two-candle pattern. Harami in Japanese is a term used for a pregnant woman.

This pattern occurs when there is a doji candle formed within the body of the previous day's candle (Chart 11.10). The type of the previous day's candle will decide whether the pattern is a bullish harami pattern or a bearish harami pattern:

Thus:

- If a bullish white candle is followed by a doji candle, which is within the body of the white candle, it is a bullish harami pattern.
- Conversely, if a bearish black candle is followed by a doji candle which is within the body of the black candle, it is a bearish harami pattern.

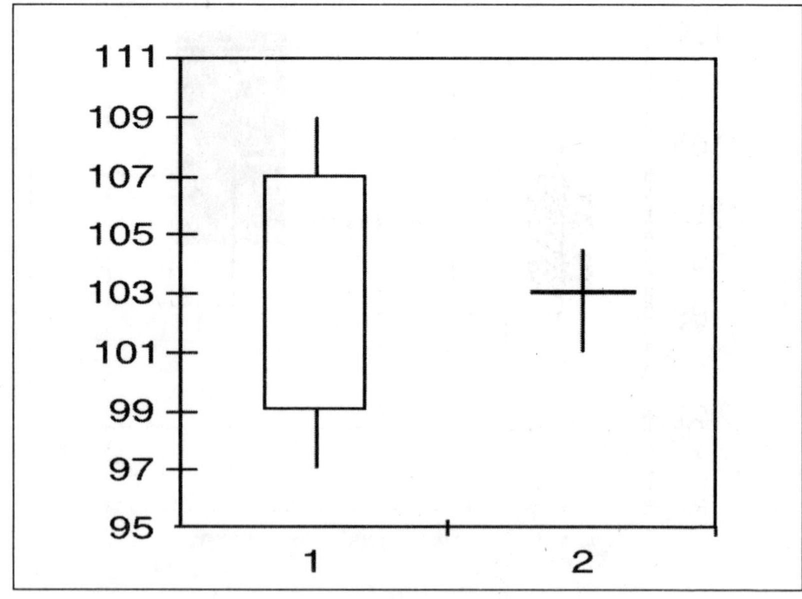

Chart 11.10: **The Harami pattern**

The Morning Star Pattern

This is a three-candle pattern (Chart 11.11). It is an important trend reversal pattern and more powerful than other reversal patterns.

The morning star pattern usually occurs when the prices have been in a down trend. Accordingly, the first candle of this pattern is a black candle indicating that the market is continuing its weakness, like on the earlier days. The second candle of this pattern is a doji, suggesting that the market is now un-decided about whether to go down further or not. The third day's candle is a white candle suggesting that the market has now decided (after the previous days' indecision) that it will go up (see Chart 11.11).

Using the filtering approach for entering a trade, it may be prudent to go long (buy) only on the fourth day — namely, the day after the white candle is formed — if the price rises above the high of the white candle.

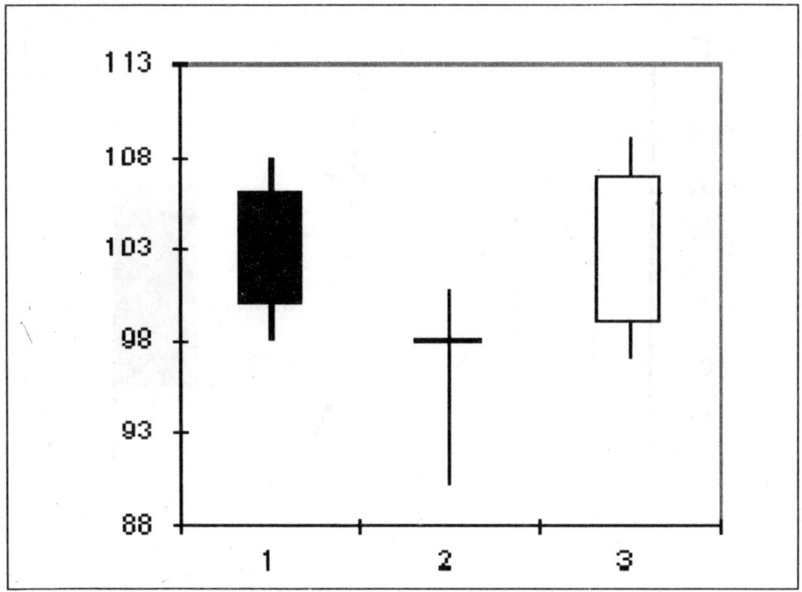

Chart 11.11: **The Morning Star pattern**

The Evening Star Pattern

This three-candle pattern is the converse of the morning star pattern and usually occurs when the price has been in an up trend.

Accordingly, the first candle of this pattern is a white candle indicating the prevailing up trend. The first candle shows that the market is continuing its bullishness like on earlier days. The second candle of this pattern is a doji, suggesting that the market has now turned un-decided about whether to rally further or not. The third day's candle is a black candle suggesting that the market has now decided (after previous days' indecision) to go down (*see* Chart 11.12).

Using the filtering approach for entering a trade, it would be prudent to go short (sell) only on the fourth day — namely, the day after the black candle is formed — if the price falls below the low of the black candle.

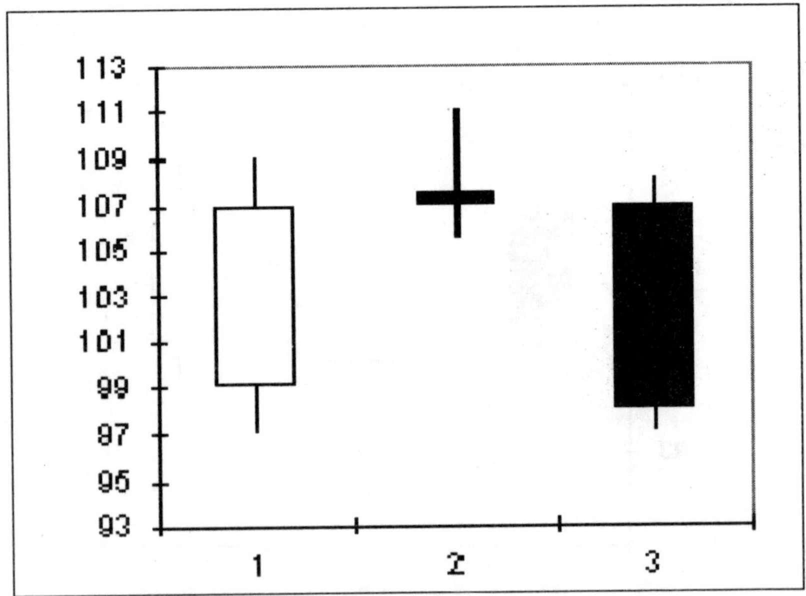

Chart 11.12: **The Evening Star pattern**

Conclusion

While these are the basic candlestick patterns and are useful for understanding market behavior, there are many more candlestick patterns which are beyond the scope of this introductory book. In fact, at the basic understanding level, the aforementioned patterns are adequate and can provide a preliminary working knowledge of the subject.

When starting out, the reader may use this knowledge of Japanese candlesticks to corroborate the results from the other tools of technical analysis covered in the previous chapters. For instance, if near the end of a down trend, the analyst finds a positive divergence on an indicator (say the RSI or MACD) and simultaneously the candlestick chart formed is of a bullish engulfing pattern or a morning star pattern, we can say that there is additional supportive confirmation, which would increase the confidence in the trade to be entered.

12

The Importance of Emotional Maturity

'When people are free to do as they please, they will usually imitate each other.'

– Eric Hoffer

I have now been in the investment business for closing to two decades and during these years I have observed various kinds of traders and investors. I have seen scalpers (intraday traders who trade for thin spreads), day traders, arbitrageurs, the short term or momentum investors, long term investors, brokers, etc. Each category has its individual characteristics and typical patterns of trading and investing.

Scalpers or day traders as a category provides an observer the maximum insight into a trader's personal traits. The euphoria when they make a profitable trade, the ecstasy when their stock hits upper circuits, their acute nervousness during the trade, and the 'world-is-against-me' feeling if they have to exit with a huge loss — all of these traits are exemplified by the scalpers.

Though in varying degrees, these traits are present in all categories of traders and investors. Even fund managers and institutional investors too have these traits, though some of them may be more successful in concealing them.

What can we learn — or unlearn — from such behavior? Emotional maturity is as important as trading discipline and an awareness of behavior traits and trading pitfalls will alert you about avoidable mistakes.

Trait 1: Lack of Mastery Over Emotions

Have you ever visited a broker's office? Especially the well-furnished, designated room having a large LCD display screen and chairs arranged to create the atmosphere of a movie theatre? If not, you should make at least one such visit.

You would see a battalion of traders, mostly scalpers, continuously glued to the LCD screen which displays the price movement of various scrips with a time lag of less than ten seconds! What is most striking is not the price fluctuations themselves, but the reactions of traders to these price fluctuations.

When they are buying and their scrip price rises even by one rupee, they feel elated and confident that they are on the right track. But if the price falls even by twenty-five paisa from their buying price, this same emotion turns to fear.

Often, these emotions are openly displayed — whether as a shout of glee, or a clap, or a groan, depending on the price fluctuation, even by people with otherwise calm temperaments.

An important learning from this trait is that one must learn to be calmer, be a master of one's emotions and get used to the seemingly erratic price swings. The fallout of ignoring this is the likelihood of higher stress level which will both lead to confused thinking and even health risks.

Trait 2: Seeking Opinion at the Wrong Time

A common bad habit that traders develop in the initial phase of their careers is that of seeking opinion at the wrong time. No, don't get this wrong. I am not at all against seeking opinion. In fact, novices in this field must seek expert opinion.

The problem lies elsewhere. Most traders will seek opinion, whether from their brokers or consultants, after they've already entered into a trading position and most likely when the market has gone against them. You may take the opinions of experts and friends, but seek it before you make a trade, not afterwards.

In fact, such post-trade opinion-seeking clearly reveals that the trader was not sure of his expected risk and return when he entered the trade. Thus, the starting point of the trade itself was faulty, which is then sought to be overcome by seeking hurried opinions as a fire-fighting measure.

A corollary to this is the pitfall of seeking opinion from too many people. Remember, there will be as many opinions as there are players. The more people you ask about a stock or the market, the more confused you will get. In fact, many a time this may even prevent you from entering into a trade!

Beware of this pitfall before it is too late. Always seek expert opinion before you enter a trade, and not afterwards. And don't get paralyzed by seeking opinions from too many people.

Trait 3: Inability to Take Losses

There is an open secret about consultants — especially investment consultants. Whenever investors make money based on their consultant's suggestion, more than half the credit for the gain goes to the market, the company, the general sentiment, the good economic fundamentals. But the moment an investor loses any money as a result of his consultant's recommendation, all hell is let loose upon the latter. He is squarely blamed for not being vigilant, knowledgeable, or alert enough. This particular trait is more visible among investors though some traders too have their share of it. When their trade results in a profit, they pat themselves feeling that they have 'mastered' the movement of the market or the scrip. They feel hugely confident and even start offering opinion to other fellow traders on their positions, most of the time even when not asked for.

But the moment one of their trades goes bad, they start complaining loudly about how poorly the stock exchange authorities are working, how speculators are not brought to book, how corrupt the regulators have become, how insiders are playing with the stock, and so on. They heap blame on all and sundry instead of accepting their own responsibility.

In truth, there is only one person responsible for your profits and losses — and that is you, yourself. To be successful in the stock market, you have to accept responsibility for your losses.

Trait 4: Trying to Kiss All the Girls

Now, don't take that literally.

Most day traders and scalpers tend to trade in and out of a large number of securities — many a time more than seven to ten in a day, hoping that profits from some trades will offset any losses from the others. In the process the only person who gains is their broker.

They may convince themselves that they are diversifying their portfolio. But in essence they are taking the diversification theory too far. Most such 'bungee jumping' happens when they discover to their dismay that some other scrip is showing stronger movement than the scrip they are trading. They immediately shift to the 'moving' scrip, getting out of the non-moving one. With this sort of jumping from scrip to scrip the whole day, one can end up trading in ten scrips (or even fifteen) during the day.

The point to learn here is that it may be prudent to trade in a pre-selected limited number of scrips rather than trying to 'kiss all the girls!'. There is a distinct advantage in being selective and focused. When you trade only in a limited number of scrips, especially using price charting techniques explained in earlier chapters, chances are that you will know more about each one of them and will be better able to understand their price behavior.

Long time professional traders are known to have the ability to even anticipate the next advances of their chosen scrips. This ability comes from closely and thoroughly following only a few securities.

Trait 5: Having a Buy Bias

Have you ever noticed that most investors are more comfortable and amenable to 'buy' recommendations than to 'sell' ones? If ten buying recommendations are flashed on a popular television channel, chances are that traders will take note and trade in most of them. But when the same channel flashes sell recommendations traders would typically not even act on half of them.

Investors and traders have an inherent tendency to trade on the long side. I have found this even among day traders who are supposed to trade as per the trend; yet most of their trades are on the long side. This is true even on days when markets are weak or negative.

This could be because of the widespread perception that security prices are 'supposed' to generally go up and not down. But security prices do go down and often for several months, or even years.

Thus, it is important for a trader to trade both sides without bias. Continuing your trades only on the buy side (or only on the sell side) would lead to sub-optimal results. A trader should not be concerned whether the market is going up or down so long as he is on its right side of it. He is there to make money from the price action taking place — and price action could, and, will, always be two-way.

Trait 6: Inability to Accept a Mistake

You could, inevitably, make some mistakes whenever you trade. This is because, as often mentioned in this book, you are essentially dealing with the future which is unpredictable. And when dealing with uncertain situations, you are bound to go wrong sometimes.

Your aim as a trader should be to minimize the number of wrong trades and maximize the number of profitable ones. This ability of a trader is what separates trading from gambling. In gambling, the chances of an outcome occurring is 50:50 and these odds cannot be altered; in trading, however, you can increase your odds of winning.

Most investors too make the mistake of not accepting a wrong investment decision. They will somehow try to convince themselves that their decision was right and, worse still, they will try to buy the stock on its way down — a sure way of losing even more of your money. Never average down. If you are wrong — whether you are a trader or an investor — learn to accept the situation, exit the trade, and take a fresh and rational view of the market. Those who don't will experience a continuous erosion of their trading capital.

Millions of investors 'averaged down' their investments in the information-communication-entertainment (ICE) sector during the entire meltdown from March 2000. Those investors who realized that the market had turned adverse and exited were far better off than those who held on and averaged down, only to sell off much later in panic.

Though a difficult discipline to master, it is all the more useful to have the ability to accept mistakes and start anew than to hold on to a wrong trade and increase both your losses and blood pressure levels!

Trait 7: The Compulsive Urge to Trade All the Time

I have observed many traders, especially day traders, have this inner urge to trade even though they may not have adequate trading signals or other reason to do so. Somehow they have a notion that since they have come to the broker's terminal, they must trade.

Believe me, many a time the best trading decision you can take is not to trade. Yes, there are many days when the markets go into slumber and become directionless. Or many a time the price does not conform with your defined trade entry parameters. Nevertheless, this inner urge seems to prompt many traders to jump in and trade in anticipation of a move.

This can be a big mistake. My experience has been that whenever a trader enters a trade in anticipation he is taking far too much risk. It is always better to trade based on clear signals — it's better not to trade if you don't find a clear logic for doing so.

Conclusion

There are many other definable traits which you will encounter in your trading career. Some of these will be specific to you while others (like those mentioned above) may be more widely prevalent.

It is important for any trader, whether a beginner or a seasoned one, to be aware of one's emotions. 'Know thyself' is the relevant mantra. Over a period you observe yourself trading the markets, you will soon start understanding your emotions and behavior better, which will help you in achieving success not only in the markets but also in life.

Above all, let us all resolve to keep in check the triad of destructive emotions — Hope, Fear and Greed — which can lead us badly astray.

Appendix 1

Quick Guide to Charting Software

With the widespread usage of computers, it has now become not only convenient but also cost effective to use charting software. There are many such software available, and most of the features available are more or less common, often with only minor cosmetic variations.

As a user of price charts, it will be important to not only have good software but also one where data updation is easy, consistent and reliable.

There are many pirated versions of charting software available but I would strongly recommend that you buy a licensed version of the software you choose.

Also beginners do not require advanced charting software. There are some available with 'artificial intelligence', etc. but I would suggest that for a novice, the basic end-of-day model is the best to start with.

I have listed below names of some popular charting software, which are quite adequate for a beginner.

Trend Software

Throughout this book, I have used this software for illustration purpose.

This is an end-of-day charting software which updates data every day. It is a product of Reliable Software Systems Pvt Ltd., Mumbai. You can get more details from their website www.reliable.co.in.

Updation too is easy as data files can be downloaded from the company's website, or through a 'data updater' software given during installation.

Trend provides data for not only Indian stocks (BSE and NSE) but also for international stocks and indices as well for internationally traded commodities like gold, silver, crude oil, etc. and for major currencies, including rupee-dollar.

Metastock

Metastock is a popular software and comes in many versions but for beginners I would suggest using the basic end-of-day Metastock. As indicated, most of the tools, indicators and facilities will be similar as in other software products with some cosmetic changes.

In India, Viratech Software is the authorized dealer and can be reached at www.viratechindia.com.

Icharts

This is another end-of-day software which is available from www.icharts.in. For some basic indicators and technical parameters, the website allows free usage. The only negative is that analyzed charts cannot be saved, as is possible in the purchased (licensed) versions.

Chart Alert

Another end-of-day software which is available from Turnbull Advisory Pvt Ltd. Details of the software can be obtained at www.chartalert.com.

You may note that this is not an exhaustive list but only a suggestive one. I have personally used Metastock, Trend and Falcon software (also from the makers of Trend).

Most of the software mentioned above are priced below ₹ 10,000 per annum. However, you are requested to contact their individual vendors for exact quotes.

Even the websites of the stock exchanges — www.bseindia.com and www.nseindia.com provide charting facilities. But they would have their own limitations over the purchased versions.

Keep in mind the following points when you purchase any charting software:

1. It should be easy to install. Indeed, software today are easy to install on a normal configuration computer.

2. It should have a user's manual so that you can make full use of the various facilities tools and indicators available.

3. Most software have a query module which helps traders to run a query based on user-defined technical parameters. For instance, you can query for a list of stocks which have crossed their 200 DMA in the last five days, or those stocks where the RSI has become overbought, and so on.

4. Data updation on a daily basis must be consistently available. This is especially applicable for active traders.

5. Facility to save your analysis in the form of templates. Most software today provides this facility.

Appendix 2

Some Useful Books and Websites

1. Achelis, Steven B., *Technical Analysis from A to Z,* Vision Books.
2. Lefevre, Edwin., *Reminiscences of a Stock Operator,* John Wiley & Sons Inc.
3. Morris, Gregory L., *Candlestick Charting Explained,* Vision Books.
4. Pring, Martin., *Martin, Pring on Market Momentum,* Vision Books

You may also refer to the following websites dealing with technical analysis.

1. www.stockcharts.com
2. www.tradingcharts.com
3. www.investopedia.com
4. www.incrediblecharts.com
5. www.freecharts.com
6. www.traders.com
7. www.in.finance.yahoo.com

Index